Plan Now.
Retire Well.

DAVID S. CORMAN & MATTHEW E. CORMAN
Generations Advisory Group

David S. Corman & Matthew E. Corman / Generations Advisory Group
45 Braintree Hill Office Park, Suite 302
Braintree, MA 02184
https://generationsadvisorygroup.com/

Book layout ©2020 Advisors Excel, LLC

Plan Now. Retire Well. / David S. Corman & Matthew E. Corman. 1st ed.

ISBN 9798689938356

Table of Contents

The Importance of Planning

I n our firm, we've seen the result of great preparation for retirement, but, all too often, we see people who haven't given a second thought to retiring well.

It is said the average person puts more effort into planning for a vacation than they do retirement. When you're planning for a vacation, there's much to consider. For instance, where are you going? How are you getting there? What activities will you partake in once you're there? What to eat? What to pack? There are also financial considerations, like what does our budget allow? Most people know which bases to cover when it comes to going on their next vacation—often in great detail.

When it comes to retirement, however, besides just saving more money in a 401(k), IRA, etc., many people are either too overwhelmed to know where to begin or choose to keep kicking the can down the road instead of addressing all the important aspects of retirement. We'll address these topics in this book.

First, here are a few cautionary tales of those who did not plan to fail, but failed to plan.

Risk in Investments – Mr. and Mrs. Schlesener met and fell in love while working at Polaroid, one of America's leading companies at the time. Both were about the same age, and they were planning on retiring at sixty-five. When Mr. and Mrs. Schlesener began to look toward retirement in the nineties, their life savings were all in Polaroid stock! They had well over $700,000 and were very proud of what they had accumulated.

What the Schleseners didn't realize is how they were exhibiting a typical case of having "all your eggs in one basket."

Sadly for Mr. and Mrs. Schlesener, the demise of Polaroid came fast and furious and, for them, at the worst possible time. Just as they were about to retire, the value of their life's work had evaporated from a very healthy $700,000 down to just over $50,000.

While Mr. and Mrs. Schlesener had accumulated money during their lifetime, they had become emotionally attached to a piece of paper (their stock in Polaroid) and thought the party would last forever. They didn't consider what might happen if things didn't go their way. This is why it's so important to not just amass money but to consider risk and other conflicting factors.

Long-Term Care Exposure – Mr. and Mrs. Falley grew up in Boston. The children of hardworking immigrants from the old country, they were no strangers to hard work themselves. From the age of sixteen until sixty-five, they managed to raise and educate five children, buy a house, pay off their mortgage, save for retirement, and pay their taxes. Needless to say, most would say they did all the right things. Mr. Falley even had a pension, and they had managed to purchase a small condo in Florida, which they would visit on annual vacations.

One day, our office received a call from Mr. and Mrs. Falley's oldest daughter, who we knew growing up. In a panic, she informed us that her dad had just experienced a debilitating stroke, and Mrs. Falley couldn't take care of him any longer. At age seventy-one, Mr. and Mrs. Falley's lives, as they had known it, changed overnight. A little prudent and pre-emptive planning would have gone a long way.

Within four years, virtually their entire nest egg went to the long-term care facility where Mr. Falley ended up living. They even had to sell their condo. If Mr. and Mrs. Falley had come in prior to retiring, we could have put a simple, but effective, plan into place that could have prevented them from having to drain their life savings on long-term care.

The common theme with these cautionary tales: These families didn't plan to fail at all, but they did fail to plan. With just a little effort, they could have had a plan that addressed the impediments to a successful retirement they experienced. Believe it or not, it's totally worth a small amount of time to have a plan addressing the most ruinous causes of financial worry.

Just saying, "I have enough money," is not a plan.

Imagine living retirement on your own terms, knowing you won't have to worry about finances. The impact of market downturns or health concerns shouldn't have to scare you.

By working with Generations Advisory Group, our clients build a comprehensive plan which addresses things many people know but also covers the things that a lot of people may not think about until it's too late.

CHAPTER 1

Longevity

Y ou would think the prospect of the grave would loom more frightening as we age, yet many retirees say their number one fear is actually running out of money in their twilight years.[1] This fear is, unfortunately, justified, in part, because of one significant factor: We're living longer.

According to the Social Security Administration, in 1950, the average life expectancy for a sixty-five-year-old man was seventy-eight, and the average for a sixty-five-year-old woman was eighty-one. In 2020, those averages were eighty-three and eighty-eight, respectively.[2]

The bottom line of many retirees' budget woes comes down to this: They just didn't plan to live so long. Now, when we are younger and in our working years, that's not something we necessarily see as a bad thing; don't some people fantasize about living forever or, at least, reaching the ripe old age of one hundred?

However, with a longer lifespan, as we near retirement, we face a few snags. Our resources are finite—we only have so much money to provide income—but our lifespans can be

---

[1] Samiha Khanna. Journal of Accountancy. February 14, 2019. "Clients' Top Fear: Running out of Money."
https://www.journalofaccountancy.com/news/2019/feb/top-retirement-fears-201920387.html
[2] Social Security Administration. 2011 Trustees Report. "Actuarial Publications: Cohort Life Expectancy."
https://www.ssa.gov/OACT/TR/2011/lr5a4.html

unpredictably long, perhaps longer than our resources allow. Also, longer lives don't necessarily equate with healthier lives. The longer you live, the more money you will likely need to spend on health care, even excluding long-term care needs like nursing homes.

You will also run into inflation. If you don't plan to live another twenty-five years but end up doing so, inflation at an average 2.5 percent will raise your $50,000-per-year budgeted need up to $93,000 per year. Or, if you live another eight years as inflation rises, you will need about $810,000 to cover those same expenses.[3] And this is before you count the expenses of any potential health care or long-term care needs.

Because we don't necessarily get to have our cake and eat it, too, our collective increased longevity hasn't necessarily increased the healthy years of our lives. Typically, our life-extending care most widely applies to the time in our lives where we will need more care in general. Think of common situations like a pacemaker at eighty-five, or cancer treatment at seventy-eight.

"Wow, David and Matthew," we can hear you say. "Way to start with the good news first."

We know, we've painted a grim picture. But all we're concerned about here is the cost. It's hard to put a dollar sign on life, but that is essentially what we're talking about when discussing longevity and your finances. According to the Stanford Center on Longevity, more than half of pre-retirees underestimate the life expectancy of the average sixty-five-year-old.[4] Living longer isn't a bad thing; it just costs more, and one key to a sound retirement strategy is preparing in advance for that expense.

---

[3] Katie Brockman. The Motley Fool. August 19, 2018. "More Americans are Living into Their 90s—and That's Bad News for Their Savings." https://www.fool.com/retirement/2018/08/19/more-americans-are-living-into-their-90s-and-thats.aspx

[4] Stanford Center on Longevity. "Underestimating Years in Retirement." http://longevity.stanford.edu/underestimating-years-in-retirement/

It's been our experience over the years that there are certain things we can control and some we can't. Genetics fall under what we can't control. For example, one of our very first clients passed away a few years back at the age of ninety-eight. While she lived a long life, she outlived all her friends. Her son, who certainly had a healthy family history and exercised regularly, unfortunately was diagnosed with cancer and passed away at the age of sixty-three, when our client was ninety-four and still going strong.

We've seen it the other way around, too. We have a client who just turned ninety, and he still goes on daily walks and insists on mowing his own lawn. He's even just as sharp as the day we met nearly twenty-five years ago! Both his parents, however, didn't make it beyond age sixty. It goes to show you, although genetics, diet, and exercise all play a role, some things are—and always will be—out of our control.

Another woman we know of illustrates how to deal with this picture perfectly. Her mother passed away in her late seventies after years of suffering from Alzheimer's disease. Her father died at eighty from cancer. With modern medicine and treatment, this woman survived two rounds of breast cancer, lived with diabetes, and relied on a pacemaker, extending her life to age eighty-eight, nearly a decade beyond what she anticipated. However, she and her husband had saved and planned for "just in case," trying to be prepared if they had to move, needed nursing home care, or needed to help children and grandchildren with their expenses. One of their "just-in-case" scenarios was living much longer than they anticipated. The last six years of her life were fraught with medical expenses, but she was also blessed with knowing her five great-grandchildren and deepening relationships with her children and grandchildren. She was able to pay for her own medical care, including her final two years in a nursing home, and her twilight years were truly golden.

From age eighty-five to eighty-eight, she was more socially active, with many visits from family and friends. She participated in more activities than she had in the seven years since her husband died. Her planning from decades earlier allowed her to pass on a legacy to her children when she passed away herself. The legacy she left behind can be measured both in dollar signs *and* in other intangible ways.

Living longer may be more expensive, but it can be so meaningful when you plan for your "just-in-cases."

Retiring Later

Planning for a long life in retirement partly depends on when you retire. While many people end up retiring earlier than they anticipated—due to injuries, layoffs, family crises, and other unforeseen circumstances—continuing to work past age sixty (and even sixty-five) is still a viable option for others and can be an excellent way to help establish financial comfort in retirement.

There are many reasons for this. For one, you obviously still earn a paycheck and the benefits accompanying it. Medical coverage and beefing up your retirement accounts with further savings can be significant by themselves but continuing your income also should keep you from dipping into your retirement funds, further allowing them the opportunity to grow.

Additionally, for many workers, their nine-to-five job is more than just clocking in and out. Having a sense of purpose can keep us active physically, mentally, and socially. That kind of activity and level of engagement may also help stave off many of the health problems that plague retirees. Avoiding a sedentary life is one of the advantages of staying plugged into the workforce, if possible.

We recently had a friend, "Mary," who worked as a nurse from the day she graduated school until the age of sixty-three, when she was just ready to travel and see the world. She had been diligently contributing to her 401(k) and retirement accounts, and, along with her pension, had a plan with more than enough income to sustain her lifestyle so she never had to work again.

For the next two years, she traveled the world and checked off lots of items on her bucket list. She even sent us pictures of her travels through Italy, France, and the like. She told us she was "busy with things she liked to do, not just things she had to do." At first, she was concerned she wouldn't have enough to do to fill her days and boredom would creep in, but fast forward two years and she told us she doesn't know how she ever made time to work before she retired!

Health Care

Take a second to reflect on your health care plan. Although working up to or even past age sixty-five would allow you to avoid a coverage gap between your working years and Medicare, that may not be an option for you. Even if it is, when you retire, you will need to make some decisions about what kind of insurance coverage you may need to supplement your Medicare. Are there any medical needs you have that may require coverage in addition to Medicare? Did your parents or grandparents have any inherited medical conditions you might consider using a special savings plan to cover?

These are all questions that are important to review with your financial professional so you can be sure you have enough money put aside for health care.

Long-Term Care

Longevity means the need for long-term care is statistically more likely to happen. If you intend to pass on a legacy, planning for long-term care is paramount, since it's estimated that nearly 70 percent of Americans will need some type of it.[5] However, this may be one of the biggest, most stressful pieces of longevity planning we encounter in our work. For one thing, who wants to talk about the point in their lives when they may feel the most limited? Who wants to dwell on what will happen if they no longer can toilet, bathe, dress, or feed themselves?

We get it; this is a less-than-fun part of planning. But a little bit of preparation now can go a long way!

When it comes to your longevity, just like with your goals, one of the important things to do is sit and dream. It may not be the fun, road-trip-to-the-Grand-Canyon kind of dreaming, but you can spend time envisioning how you want your twilight years to look.

For instance, if it is important for you to live in your home for as long as possible, who will provide for the day-to-day fixes and to-dos of housework if you become ill? Will you set aside money for a service, or do you have relatives or friends nearby whom you could comfortably allow to help you? Do you prefer in-home care over a nursing home or assisted living? This could be a good time to discuss the possibility of moving into a retirement community versus staying where you are or whether it's worth moving to another state and leaving relatives behind.

These are all important factors to discuss with your spouse and children, as *now* is the right time to address questions and concerns. For instance, is aging in place more important to one spouse than the other? Are the friends or relatives who live nearby emotionally, physically, and financially capable of helping you for a time if you face an illness?

Many families we meet with find these conversations very uncomfortable, particularly when children discuss nursing home care with their parents. A knee-jerk reaction for many is to promise they will care for their aging parents. This is noble

---

[5] Moll Law Group. 2019. "The Cost of Long-Term Care." https://www.molllawgroup.com/the-cost-of-long-term-care.html

and well-intentioned, but there needs to be an element of realism here. Does "help" from an adult child mean they stop by and help you with laundry, cooking, home maintenance, and bills? Or does it mean they move you into their spare room when you have hip surgery? Are they prepared to help you use the restroom and bathe if that becomes difficult for you to do on your own?

We don't mean to discourage families from caring for their own; this can be a profoundly admirable relationship when it works out. However, we've seen families put off planning for late-in-life care based on a tenuous promise that the adult children would care for their parents, only to watch as the support system crumbles. Sometimes this is because the assumed caregiver hasn't given serious thought to the preparation they would need, both in a formal sense and regarding their personal physical, emotional, and financial commitments. This is often also because we can't see the future: Alzheimer's disease and other maladies of old age can exact a heavy toll. When a loved one reaches the point where he or she is at risk of wandering away or needs help with two or more activities of daily living, it can be more than one person or family can realistically handle.

If you know what you want, communicate with your family about both the best-case and worst-case scenarios. Then, hope for the best, and plan for the worst.

Realistic Cost of Care

Wrapped up in your planning should be a consideration for the cost of long-term care. Although many of us will need some degree of long-term care—including the 30 percent of us who may need up to five years of facility care—60 percent of us underestimate the costs of nursing home care. On average, consumers underestimate the annual cost of a private room in a nursing home by 51 percent.[6]

Another piece of planning for long-term care costs is anticipating inflation. It's common knowledge that prices have been and keep rising, and that will lower your purchasing power on everything from food to medical care. Long-term care is a big piece of the inflation-disparity pie, which is part of why many find their estimates of nursing home care widely miss the mark. According to one survey, people expected to pay around $25,350 in out-of-pocket long-term care expenses per year, but, in reality, they'll more likely be paying over $47,000.[7]

While local costs vary from state to state, here's the national median for various forms of long-term care (plus projections that account for a 3 percent annual inflation, so you can see what we're talking about):[8]

---

[6] Tamara E. Holmes. Yahoo Finance. July 24, 2019. "Consumers Underestimate Costs of Long-Term Care." https://finance.yahoo.com/news/consumers-underestimate-costs-long-term-173542918.html

[7] Moll Law Group. 2019. "The Cost of Long-Term Care." https://www.molllawgroup.com/the-cost-of-long-term-care.html

[8] Genworth Financial. May 2020. "Cost of Care Survey 2019." https://www.genworth.com/aging-and-you/finances/cost-of-care.html

Long-Term Care Costs: Inflation				
	Home Health Care, Homemaker Services	Adult Day Care	Assisted Living	Nursing Home (semi-private room)
Annual 2019	$51,480	$19,500	$48,612	$90,155
Annual 2029	$69,185	$26,206	$65,330	$121,161
Annual 2039	$92,979	$35,219	$87,799	$162,830
Annual 2049	$124,955	$47,332	$117,994	$218,830

While these are the national numbers, in reality, the cost of care in Massachusetts is much higher. The cost for a private room in Massachusetts routinely exceeds $155,000 per year. Ouch![9]

Fund Your Long-Term Care

One critical mistake we see are those who haven't planned for long-term care because they assume the government will provide everything. But that's a big misconception. The government has two health insurance programs: Medicare and Medicaid. These can greatly assist you in your health care needs in retirement but usually don't provide enough coverage to cover all your health care costs in retirement. Our firm isn't a government outpost, so we don't get to make decisions when it comes to forming policy and specifics about either one of these programs. We're going to give the overview of both, but

[9] Ibid.

if you want to dive into the details of these programs, you can visit www.Medicare.gov and www.Medicaid.gov.

Medicare

Medicare covers those aged sixty-five and older and those who are disabled. Medicare's coverage of any nursing-home-related health issues is limited. It might cover your nursing home stay if it is not a "custodial" stay, and it isn't long-term. For example, if you break a bone or suffer a stroke, stay in a nursing home for rehabilitative care, and then return home, Medicare may cover you. But, if you have developed dementia or are looking to move to a nursing facility because you can no longer bathe, dress, toilet, feed yourself, or take care of your hygiene, etc., then Medicare is not going to pay for your nursing home costs.[10]

Medicaid

Medicaid is a program the states administer, so funding, protocol, and limitations vary. Compared to Medicare, Medicaid more widely covers nursing home care, but it targets a different demographic than Medicare: those with low incomes.

If you have more assets than the Medicaid limit in your state and need nursing home care, you will need to use those assets to pay for your care. You will also have a list of additional state-approved ways to spend some of these assets over the Medicaid limit, such as pre-purchasing burial plots and funeral expenses or paying off debts. After that, your remaining assets fund your nursing home stay until they are gone, at which point Medicaid will jump in.

Some people aren't stymied by this, thinking they will just pass on their financial assets early, gifting them to relatives, friends, and causes so they can qualify for Medicaid when they need it. However, to prevent this exact scenario, Uncle Sam

---

[10] Medicare.gov. "What Part A covers." https://www.medicare.gov/what-medicare-covers/part-a/what-part-a-covers.html

has implemented the look-back period. Currently, if you enroll in Medicaid, you are subject to having the government scrutinize the last five years of your finances for large gifts or expenses that may subject you to penalties, temporarily making you ineligible for Medicaid coverage.

So, if you're planning to preserve your money for future generations and retain control of your financial resources during your lifetime, you'll probably want to prepare for the costs of longevity beyond a "government plan."

Self-Funding

One way to fund a longer life is the old-fashioned way, through self-funding. There are a variety of financial tools you can use, and they all have their pros and cons. If your assets are in low-interest financial vehicles (savings, bonds, CDs), you risk letting inflation erode the value of your dollar. Or, if you are relying on the stock market, you have more growth potential, but you'll also want to consider the possible implications of market volatility. What if your assets take a hit? If you suffer a loss in your retirement portfolio in early or mid-retirement, you might have the option to "tighten your belt," so to speak, and cut back on discretionary spending to allow your portfolio the room to bounce back. But, if you are retired and depend on income from a stock account that just hit a downward stride, what are you going to do?

HSAs

These days, you might also be able to self-fund through a health savings account, or HSA, if you have access to one through a high-deductible health plan (you will not qualify to save in an HSA after enrolling in Medicare). In an HSA, any growth of your tax-deductible contributions will be tax-free, and any distributions paid out for qualified health costs are also tax-free. Long-term care expenses count as health costs, so, if this is an option available to you, it is one way to use the tax advantages to self-fund your longevity. Bear in mind, if you are younger than sixty-five, any money you use for nonqualified expenses will be subject to taxes and penalties, and, if you are older than sixty-five, any HSA money you use for non-medical expenses is subject to income tax.

LTCI

One slightly more nuanced way to pay for longevity, specifically for long-term care, is long-term care insurance, or LTCI. As car insurance protects your assets in case of a car accident and home insurance protects your assets in case something happens to your house, long-term care insurance aims to protect your assets in case you need long-term care in an at-home or nursing home situation.

As with other types of insurance, you will pay a monthly or annual premium in exchange for an insurance company paying for long-term care down the road. Typically, policies cover two to three years of care, which is adequate for an "average" situation: it's estimated 70 percent of Americans will need about three years of long-term care of some kind. However, it's important to consider you might not be "average" when you are preparing for long-term care costs; on average, 20 percent of today's sixty-five-year-olds could need care for longer than five years.[11]

Now, there are a few oft-cited components of LTCI that make it unattractive for some:

- Expense — LTCI can be expensive. It is generally less expensive the younger you are, but a fifty-five-year-old couple who purchased LTCI in 2019 could expect to pay $3,050 each year for an average three-year coverage policy. And the annual cost only increases from there the older you are.12

[11] David Levine. *U.S. News.* July 10, 2019. "How to Pay for Nursing home Costs." https://health.usnews.com/best-nursing-homes/articles/how-to-pay-for-nursing-home-costs
[12] American Association for Long-Term Care Insurance. January 2019. "2019 National Long-Term Care Insurance Price Index."

- Limited options — Let's face it: LTCI may be expensive for consumers, but it can also be expensive for companies that offer it. With fewer companies willing to take on that expense, this narrows the market, meaning opportunities to price shop for policies with different options or custom benefits are limited.
- If you know you need it, you might not be able to get it — Insurance companies offering LTCI are taking on a risk that you may need LTCI. That risk is the foundation of the product—you may or may not need it. If you know you will need it because you have a dementia diagnosis or another illness for which you will need long-term care, you will likely not qualify for LTCI coverage.
- Use it or lose it—If you have LTCI and are in the minority of Americans who die having never needed long-term care, all the money you paid into your LTCI policy is gone.
- Possibly fluctuating rates—Your rate is not locked in on LTCI. Companies maintain the ability to raise or lower your premium amounts. This means some seniors face an ultimatum: Keep funding a policy at what might be a less affordable rate *or* lose coverage and let go of all the money they paid in so far.

After that, you might be thinking, "How can people possibly be interested in LTCI?" But let us repeat ourselves—as many as 70 percent of Americans will need long-term care. And, although only 8 percent of Americans have purchased LTCI, keep in mind the high cost of nursing home care. Can you afford $7,000 a month to put into nursing home care and still have enough left over to protect your legacy? This is a very real concern: One study says 72 percent of Americans are

---

https://www.aaltci.org/news/wp-content/uploads/2019/01/2019-Price-Index-LTC.pdf

impoverished by the end of just one year in a nursing home.[13] So, not to sound like a broken record, but it is vitally important to have a plan in place to deal with longevity and long-term care if you intend to leave a financial legacy.

In our experience with long-term care insurance, the marketplace has changed over the years. Nowadays, for some people, long-term care insurance could be a viable option for protecting against long-term care expenses. With LTCI, there come some pros and cons.

The Pros: You don't necessarily have to be in a long-term care facility to use the benefits. For example, many LTCI policies allow you to use benefits for home health visits, homemaker services (i.e. light cleaning), and other services designed to assist you to live at home comfortably rather than having to go into a facility. Another pro is many policies will pay for assisted living costs, provided you qualify as per the ADLs (activities of daily living).

The Cons: For one, the newer LTCI policies tend to cost even more than before. Additionally, it is more difficult to qualify in terms of health than the previous generations of policies. Lastly, in addition to cost being a main concern, with many policies, the premiums become "use it or lose it," which means, if you never end up needing the policy, that money doesn't come back to your family.

To summarize, there are two camps when it comes to LTCI. One camp believes the costs outweigh the benefits and will roll the dice without LTCI coverage. The second camp doesn't mind paying the costs simply because, if they actually end up needing the benefits, they will help with living a life of dignity without sacrificing financial independence.

---

[13] A Place for Mom. January 2018. "Long-Term Care Insurance: Costs & Benefits." http://www.aplaceformom.com/senior-care-resources/articles/long-term-care-costs.

Product Riders

LTCI and self-funding are not the only ways to plan for the expenses of longevity. Some companies are getting creative with their products, particularly insurance companies. One way they are retooling to meet people's needs is through optional product riders on annuities and life insurance. Elsewhere in this book, we talk about annuity basics, but here's a brief overview: Annuities are insurance contracts. You pay the insurance company a premium, either as a lump sum or as a series of payments over a set amount of time, in exchange for guaranteed income payments. One of the advantages of an annuity is it has access to riders, which allow you to tweak your contract for a fee, usually about 1 percent of the contract value annually. One annuity rider some companies offer is a long-term care rider. If you have an annuity with a long-term care rider and are not in need of long-term care, your contract behaves as any annuity contract would—nothing changes. Generally speaking, if you reach a point when you can't perform multiple functions of daily life on your own, you notify the insurance company, and a representative will turn on those provisions of your contract.

Like LTCI, different companies and products offer different options. Some annuity long-term care riders offer coverage of two years in a nursing home situation. Others cap expenses at two times the original annuity's value. It greatly depends. Some people prefer this option because there isn't a "use-it-or-lose-it" piece; if you die without ever having needed long-term care, you still will have had the income benefit from the base contract. Still, as with any annuities or insurance contracts, there are the usual restrictions and limitations. Withdrawing money from the contract will affect future income payments, early distributions can result in a penalty, income taxes may apply, and, because the insurance company's solvency is what guarantees your payments, it's important to do your research about the insurance company you are considering purchasing a contract from.

Understandably, a discussion on long-term care is bound to feel at least a little tedious. Yet, this is a critical piece of planning for income in retirement, particularly if you want to leave a legacy.

Based on our observations, long-term care costs are the number one drain on senior wealth.

Spousal Planning

Here's one thing to keep in mind no matter how you plan to save: Many of us will be planning for more than ourselves. Look back at all the stats on health events and the likelihood of long life and long-term care. If they hold true for a single individual, then the likelihood of having a costly health or long-term care event is even higher for a married couple. You'll be planning for not just one life, but two. So, when it comes to long-term care insurance, annuities, self-funding, or whatever strategy you are looking at using, be sure you are funding longevity for the both of you.

When we construct a plan for our clients, we factor in the very real possibility of living a long life. Importantly, though, this is not done at the expense of enjoying life early in retirement when retirees are still very active and have lots of things to do and see. The last thing anybody wants is to have to pinch pennies in fear of exhausting their lifetime of savings.

CHAPTER 2

Taxes

Where to begin with taxes? Perhaps by acknowledging we all bear responsibility for the resources we share. Roads, bridges, schools . . . It is the patriotic duty of every American to pay their fair share of taxes. Many would agree with us, though, while they don't mind paying their fair share, they're not interested in paying one cent more than that!

Now, just talking taxes probably takes your mind to April—tax season. You are probably thinking about all the forms you collect and how you file. Perhaps you are thinking about your certified public accountant or another qualified tax professional and saying to yourself, "I've already got taxes taken care of, thanks!"

However, what we see when people come into our office is that their relationship with their tax professional is purely a January through April relationship. That means they may have a tax professional, but not a tax *planner*.

What we mean is tax planning extends beyond filing taxes. In April, we are required to settle our accounts with the IRS to make sure we have paid up on our bill or to even the score if we have overpaid. But real tax planning is about making each financial move in a way that allows you to keep the most money in your pocket and out of Uncle Sam's.

Now, as a caveat, we want to emphasize we are not CPAs or tax planners, but we see the way taxes affect our clients, and we have plenty of experience helping clients implement tax-efficient strategies in their retirement plans in conjunction with their tax professionals.

It is especially important to us to help our clients develop tax-efficient strategies in their retirement plans because each dollar they can keep in their pockets is a dollar we can put to work.

For example, we had a client come in recently who had just retired and had begun to withdraw money from her 401(k) to supplement her income. In addition to her 401(k), she also had another account, a non-qualified brokerage account, from which she could withdraw income. Because she didn't have a plan for how to withdraw the money in her various accounts, she was withdrawing in a way that meant she paid in excess of $12,000 per year in unnecessary taxes. Over the course of six years, that was an excess of $75,000 that she could put back in her pocket; it could go a long way toward some nice vacations!

The Fed

Now, in the United States, taxes can be a rather uncertain proposition. Depending on who is in the White House and which party controls Congress, we might be tempted to assume tax rates could either decline or increase in the next four to eight years accordingly. However, there is one (large!) factor we, as a nation, must confront: the national debt.

Currently, according to USDebtClock.org, we are over $26,000,000,000,000 in debt and climbing. That's $26 *trillion* with a "T." With just $1 trillion, you could park it in the bank at a zero percent interest rate and still spend more than $54 million every day for fifty years without hitting a zero balance.

Even if Congress got a handle and stopped that debt from its daily compound, divided by each taxpayer, we each would owe about $200,000. So, will that be check or cash?

Our point here isn't to give you anxiety. We're just saying, even with the rosiest of outlooks on our personal income tax rates, none of us should count on low tax rates for the long term. Instead, you and your network of professionals (tax, legal, and financial) should constantly be looking for ways to take advantage of tax-saving opportunities as they come. After all, the best "luck" is when proper planning meets opportunity.

So, how can we get started?

Know Your Limits

One of the foundational pieces of tax planning is knowing what tax bracket you are in, based on your income after subtracting pre-tax or untaxed assets. Your income taxes are based on your taxable income.

One reason to know your taxable income and your income tax rate is so you can see how far away you are from the next lower or higher tax bracket. This is particularly important when it comes to decisions such as gifting and Roth IRA rollovers.

For instance, based on the 2020 tax table, Mallory and Ralph's taxable income is just over $330,000, putting them in the 32 percent tax bracket and about $3,400 above the upper end of the 24 percent tax bracket. They have already maxed out their retirement funds' tax-exempt contributions for the year. Their daughter, Gloria, is a sophomore in college. This couple could shave a considerable amount off their tax bill if they use the $3,400 to help Gloria out with groceries and school—something they were likely to do, anyway, but now can deliberately be put to work for them in their overall financial strategy.

Now, we use Mallory and Ralph only as an example—your circumstances are probably different—but we think this nicely illustrates the way planning ahead for taxes can save you money.

Assuming a Lower Tax Rate

Many people anticipate being in a lower tax bracket in retirement. It makes sense: You won't contribute to retirement funds; you'll draw from them. And you won't have all those work expenses—work clothes, transportation, etc.

Yet, do you really plan on changing your lifestyle after retirement? Do you plan to cut down on the number of times you eat out, scale back vacations, and skimp on travel?

What we see in our office is many couples spend more in the first few years, or maybe the first decade, of retirement. Sure, that may taper off later on, but usually only just in time for their budget to be hit with greater health and long-term care expenses. Do you see where this is going? Many people plan as though their taxable income will be lower in retirement and are surprised when the tax bills come in and look more or less the same as they used to. It's better to plan for the worst and hope for the best, wouldn't you agree?

401(k)/IRA

One sometimes-unexpected piece of tax planning in retirement concerns your 401(k) or IRA. Most of us have one of these accounts or an equivalent. Throughout our working lives, we pay in, dutifully socking away a portion of our earnings in these tax-deferred accounts. There's the rub: tax-deferred. Not tax-free. Very rarely is anything free of taxation when you get down to it. Using 401(k)s and IRAs in retirement is no different. The taxes the government deferred when you were in your working years are now coming due, and you will pay taxes on that income at whatever your current tax rate is.

Just to ensure Uncle Sam gets his due, the government also has a required minimum distribution, or RMD, rule. Beginning at age seventy-two, you are required to withdraw a certain minimum amount every year from your 401(k) or IRA, or else you will face a 50 percent tax penalty on any RMD monies you should have withdrawn but didn't—and that's on top of income tax.

Of course, there is also the Roth account. You can think of the difference between a Roth and a traditional retirement account as the difference between taxing the seed and taxing the harvest. Because Roths are funded with post-tax dollars, there aren't tax penalties for early withdrawals of the principal nor are there taxes on the growth after you reach age fifty-nine-and-one-half. Perhaps best of all, there are no RMDs. Of course, you must own a Roth account for a minimum of five years before you are able to take advantage of all its features.

This is one more area where it pays to be aware of your tax bracket. Some people may find it advantageous to "convert" their traditional retirement account funds to Roth account funds in a year during which they are in a lower tax bracket. Others may opt to put any excess RMDs from their traditional retirement accounts into other products, like stocks or insurance.

Does that make your head spin? Understandable. That's why it's so important to work with a financial professional and tax planner who can help you not only execute these sorts of tax-efficient strategies but also help you understand what you are doing and why.

Minimizing taxes can be the difference between being able to take a vacation, buying a car you've wanted, or gifts to grandchildren, etc. Done right over the course of your lifetime, money that ends up in your pocket and not in the government's hands can truly enhance your quality of life. There's really no need to pay a penny more than your fair share.

CHAPTER 3

Market Volatility

U p and down. Roller coaster. Merry-go-round. Bulls and bears. Peak-to-trough.

Sound familiar? This is the language we use to talk about the stock market. With volatility and spikes, even our language is jarring, bracing, and vivid.

Still, financial strategies tend to revolve around market-based products, for good reasons. For one thing, there is no other financial class that packs the same potential for growth, pound for pound, as stock-based products. Because of growth potential, inflation protection, and new opportunities, it may be unwise to avoid the market entirely.

However, along with the potential for growth is the potential for loss. Many of the people we see in our office come in still feeling burned from the market drama of 2000 to 2010. That was a rough stretch, and many of us are once-bitten-twice-shy investors, right? Not to mention the market volatility brought on by, say, an international pandemic . . .

So how do we balance these factors? How do we try to satisfy both the need for protection and the need for growth?

For one thing, it is important to recognize the value of diversity. Now, we're not just talking about the diversity of assets among different kinds of stocks, or even different kinds of stocks and bonds. That's only one kind of diversity; while important, both stocks and bonds, though different, are both still market-based products. Most market-based products, even within a diverse portfolio, tend to rise or lower as a whole, just like an incoming tide. Therefore, a portfolio diverse in only market-sourced products won't automatically protect your assets during times when the market declines.

In addition to the sort of "horizontal diversity" you have by purchasing a variety of stocks and bonds from different companies, we encourage having "vertical diversity," or diversity among asset classes. This means having different product types, including securities products, bank products, and insurance products—with varying levels of growth potential, liquidity, and protection—all in accordance with your unique situation, goals, and needs.

We've found that, while people generally understand the market has periods of ups and downs, they react much more strongly when the market goes down compared to when the market goes up. Most clients we meet with express the concern that, while they understand the market has the potential to appreciate over time, they are nearing or in retirement and don't have years or decades to wait to get back to square one if the market turns negative and stays there for a while.

When structuring our clients' assets, we have to pay particular attention to mitigating downside exposure. We are upfront about the risks of market investments, and we let our clients know that anything they structure in the market has the potential for substantial and sustained losses, even over many years. With this in mind, some clients are okay with a portion of their funds being in the market, while others might want to avoid any losses whatsoever. In the abstract, it's easy for some to say they don't mind seeing losses in a portfolio for a period of time, but, when losses actually occur in their account, they often have a sinking feeling in their gut as they suddenly discover their tolerance for risk was a lot less than they had originally surmised.

For example, one woman was two years away from retirement and wanted to structure her 401(k) and IRA accordingly. With her income and other goals in mind, she should have considered a low-risk strategy. However, she decided to keep most of her money and accounts in the market, reasoning that her rate of return was high for the last few years (after all, her most recent statement showed a 13.6 percent return over the last twelve months), so she assumed that would continue indefinitely. Six months later, the market started to head toward the negative after years on end of strong growth. She went into a state of near panic about her accounts in which she chose to ignore the risk. As the famous philosopher and boxer Mike Tyson profoundly said, "Everybody has a plan until they get punched in the mouth."

The Color of Money

When you're looking at the overall diversity of your portfolio, part of the equation is knowing which products fit in what category: what has liquidity, what has protection, and what has growth potential.

Before we dive in, keep in mind these aren't absolutes. You might think of liquidity, growth, and protection as primary colors. While some products will look pretty much yellow, red, or blue, others will have a mix of characteristics, making them more green, orange, or purple.

Growth

We like to think of the growth category as red. It's powerful, it's somewhat volatile, and it's also the category where we have the greatest opportunities for growth and loss. Often, products in the growth category will have a good deal of liquidity but very little protection. These are our market-based products and strategies, and we think of them mostly in shades of red and orange, to designate their growth and liquidity. This is a good place to be when you're young—think fast cars and flashy leather jackets—but its allure often wanes as you move closer to retirement.

Examples of "red" products include:
- Stocks
- Equities
- Exchange-traded funds
- Mutual funds
- Corporate bonds
- Real estate investment trusts
- Speculations
- Alternative investments

Liquidity

Yellow is our liquid category color. We typically recommend having at least enough yellow money to cover six months' to a year's worth of expenses in case of emergency. Yellow assets don't need a lot of growth potential; they just need to be readily available when we need them. The "yellow" category includes:
- Cash
- Money market accounts

Protection

The color of protection, to us, is blue. Tranquil, peaceful, sure, even if it lacks a certain amount of flash. This is the direction we like to see people generally move toward as they're nearing retirement. The red, flashy look of stock market returns and the risk of possible overnight losses is less attractive as we near retirement and look for more consistency and reliability. While this category doesn't come with a lot of liquidity, the products here are backed by an insurance company, a bank, or a government entity. "Blue" products include:
- Certificates of deposit (FDIC-insured)
- Government-based bonds (government-backed)

- Life insurance (financial strength of the insurance carrier)
- Annuities (financial strength of the insurance carrier)

Heading into retirement and beyond, for almost everyone, income is the number one financial priority—as it should be. When we work with clients to determine a plan and course of action, we have a simple but effective two-step philosophy.

First, we work with clients to determine their income needs and then put together a plan to help meet these needs. While we will discuss the particulars of income in more detail later, the guaranteed income sources we focus on might include Social Security, pensions, and fixed/guaranteed products.

Second, once we've established an income plan, we take a look at structuring any assets above and beyond what are allocated toward funding that income plan. Here is where market-based products might or might not come into the mix, depending on the client's tolerance for risk. As we've previously noted, the client could decide they want to invest this amount in market-based products for potential higher returns, at the risk of potential losses, for a short or sustained time. On the other hand, if they decide they don't want to subject these "growth" funds to potential losses, we would then make recommendations accordingly.

401(k)s

We want to take a second to specifically address a product many retirees will be using to build their retirement income: the 401(k) and other retirement accounts. Any of these retirement accounts (IRAs, 401(k)s, 403(b)s, etc.) are basically "tax wrappers." What do we mean by that? Well, depending on your plan provider, a 401(k) could include target-date funds, passively managed products, stocks, bonds, mutual funds, or even variable, fixed, and fixed index annuities, all collected in one place and governed by rules (a.k.a. the "tax wrapper"). These rules govern how much money you can put inside, what ways you can put it in, when you will pay taxes on it, and when you can take the money out. Inside the 401(k), each of the products inside the "tax wrapper" might have its own fees or commissions, in addition to the management fee you pay on the 401(k) itself.

Now, fees can be troublesome. You can't get something for nothing, and fees are how many financial companies and professionals make a living. Yet, it's important to recognize even a fee of a single percentage point is money out of your pocket—money that represents not just the one-time fee of today but also represents an opportunity cost. One study found a single percentage point fee could cost a millennial close to $600,000 over forty years of saving.[14] For someone closer to retirement, how much do you think fees may have cost?

Even for those close to retirement, it's important to look at management fees and assess if you think you're getting what you pay for. Over the course of ten years, those puppies can add up, and you may have decades ahead of you in which you will need to rely on your assets.

Dollar-Cost Averaging

With 401(k)s and other market-based retirement products, when you are investing for the long term, dollar-cost averaging is a concept that can work in your favor. When the market is trending up, your investments can grow and you are adding to your assets, month over month, great; your investments are growing, and you are adding to your assets. When the market takes a dip, no problem; your dollars buy

---

[14] Dayana Yochim and Jonathan Todd. NerdWallet. "How a 1% Fee Could Cost Millennials $590,000 in Retirement Savings."
https://www.nerdwallet.com/blog/investing/millennial-retirement-fees-one-percent-half-million-savings-impact/

more shares at a lower price. At some point, we hope the market will rebound, in which case your money can grow and possibly be more valuable than they were before. This concept is what we call dollar-cost averaging. While it can't ensure a profit or guarantee against losses, it's a time-tested strategy for investing in a volatile market.

However, when you are in retirement, this strategy may work against you. You may have heard of "reverse" dollar-cost averaging. Before, when the market lost ground, you were "bargain-shopping"; your dollars purchased more assets at a reduced price. When you are in retirement, you are no longer the purchaser; you are selling. So, in a down market, you have to sell more assets to make the same amount of money as what you made in a favorable market.

We've had lots of people step into our office to talk to us about this, emphasizing "my advisor says the market always bounces back, and we have to just hold on for the long term."

There's some basis for this thinking; thus far, the market has always rebounded to higher heights than before. But this is no guarantee, and the prospect of potentially higher returns in five years may not be very helpful in retirement if you are relying on the income from those returns to pay this month's electric bill, for example.

While the market might do very well over time, most people come in with income as their number one priority. That's why we lean toward implementing a rock-solid and reliable income strategy first, along with principal protection, and then, only when income is secured, do we look at market-based products.

Is There a "Perfect" Product?

To bring us back around to the discussion of protection, growth, and liquidity, the ideal product would be a "ten" in all three categories, right? Completely guaranteed, doubling in size every few years, and accessible whenever you want. Does such a product exist? Anyone who says, "yes" is either ignorant or malevolent.

Instead of running in circles looking for that perfect product, the silver bullet, the unicorn of financial strategies, it's more important to circle back to the concept of a balanced, asset-diverse portfolio.

This is why your interests may be best served when you work with a trusted financial professional who knows what various financial products can do and how to use them in your personal retirement plan.

CHAPTER 4

Retirement Income

R etirement. For many of us, it's what we've saved for and dreamed of, pinning our hopes to a magical someday. Is that someday full of traveling? Is it filled with grandkids? Gardening? Maybe your fondest dream is simply never having to work again, never having to clock in or be accountable to someone else.

Your ability to do these things all hinges on *income*. Without the money to support these dreams, even a basic level of work-free lifestyle is unsustainable. That's why planning for your income in retirement is so foundational. But where do we begin?

It's easy to feel overwhelmed by this question. Some may feel the urge to amass a large lump sum and then try to put it all in one product—insurance, investments, liquid assets—to provide all the growth, liquidity, and income they need. Instead, we think you need a more balanced approach. After all, retirement planning isn't magic. As we mention elsewhere, there is no single product that can be all things to all people (or even all things to one person). No approach works unilaterally for everyone. That's why it's important to talk to a financial professional who can help you lay down the basics and take you step-by-step through the planning process. Not only will you have the assurance that you have addressed the areas you need to, but you will also have an ally who can help you break down the process and help keep you from feeling overwhelmed.

Sources of Income

Thinking of all the pieces of your retirement expenses might be intimidating. But, like cleaning out a junk drawer or revisiting that garage remodel, once you have laid everything out, you can begin to sort things into categories.

Once you have a good overall picture of where your expenses will lie, you can start stacking up the resources to cover them.

Social Security

Social Security is a guaranteed, inflation-protected federal insurance program playing a significant part in most of our retirement plans. From delaying until you've reached full retirement age or beyond to examining spousal benefits, as we discuss elsewhere in this book, there is plenty you can do to try to make the most of this monthly benefit. As with all your retirement income sources, it's important to consider how to make this resource stretch to provide the most bang and buck for your situation.

Pension

Another generally reliable source of retirement income for you might be a pension, if you are one of the lucky people who still has one.

If you don't have a pension, go ahead and skim on to the next section. If you do have a pension, keep on reading.

Because your pension can be such a central piece of your retirement income plan, you will want to put some thought into answering basic questions about it.

How well is your pension funded? Since the heyday of the pension plan, companies and governments have neglected to fund their pension obligations, causing a persistent problem with this otherwise reliable asset. Public pensions face a collective $4.7 trillion deficit, according to the U.S. Pension Tracker..[15] The Public Benefit Guaranty Association, which helps insure private pensions, reports that there is a $54 billion shortfall in multiemployer plans, affecting half of all multiemployer plans.[16] If you have a pension, it is quite possibly included in those statistics.

In addition to checking up on your pension's health, check into what your options are for withdrawing your pension. If you have already retired and made those decisions, this may be a foregone conclusion. If not, it pays to know what you can expect and what decisions you can make, such as taking spousal options to cover your husband or wife if he or she outlives you.

Also, some companies are incentivizing lump-sum payouts of pensions to reduce the companies' payment liabilities. If that's the case with your employer, talk to your financial professional to see if it might be prudent to do something like that or if it might be better to stick with lifetime payments or other options.

Your 401(k) and IRA

One "modern way" to save for retirement is in a 401(k) or IRA (or their nonprofit or governmental equivalents). These tax-advantaged accounts are, in our opinion, a poor substitute for pensions, but one of the biggest disservices we do to ourselves is to not take full advantage of them in the first place. According to one article, about 42 percent of adults under

---

[15] U.S. Pension Tracker. April 2019. us.pensiontracker.org

[16] Alessandro Malito. MarketWatch. December 11, 2018. "The Truth About Pensions: They Aren't Dead, But Some Are Barely Holding On." https://www.marketwatch.com/story/the-truth-about-pensions-they-arent-dead-but-some-are-barely-holding-on-2018-12-11

thirty and 26 percent of adults thirty to forty-four haven't contributed to any retirement account, let alone their 401(k).[17]

Also, if you have changed jobs over the years, do the work of tracking down any benefits from your past employers. You might have an IRA here or a 401(k) there; keep track of those so you can pull them together and look at those assets when you're ready to look at establishing sources of retirement income.

Do You Have...

- Life insurance?
- Annuities?
- Long-term care insurance?
- Any passive income sources?
- Stock and bond portfolios?
- Liquid assets? (What's in your bank account?)
- Alternative investments?
- Rental properties?

It's important, if you are going through the work of sitting with a financial professional, to look at your full retirement income picture and pull together *all* your assets, no matter how big or small. From the free insurance policy offered at your bank to the sizable investment in your brother-in-law's modestly successful furniture store, you want to have a good idea of where your money is.

Years of savings and compounding interest can really add up. Many people are surprised as to how much they really have saved. There could be an IRA here, an old 401(k) there, and savings in a couple different banks. Most people are busy living their lives and not calculating net worth and investment

---

[17] Niall McCarthy. Forbes. June 3, 2019. "Report: A Quarter of Americans Have No Retirement Savings."
https://www.forbes.com/sites/niallmccarthy/2019/06/03/report-a-quarter-of-americans-have-no-retirement-savings-infographic/#5fb35b703ebf

returns. But the combination of saving diligently year after year, along with compounded growth (and, many times, the value of their homes), many people can be surprised how much they are really worth! Especially combined with Social Security or pensions, many people are surprised how much income they can really generate while retired.

Retirement Income Needs

How much income will you need in retirement? How do you determine that? A lot of people work toward a random number, thinking, "If I can just have a million dollars, I'll be comfortable in retirement!" Don't get us wrong; it is possible to save up a lot of money and then retire in the hopes you can keep your monthly expenses lower than some set estimation. But we think this carries a general risk of running out of money. Instead, we work with our clients to find out what their current and projected income needs are and then work from there to see how we might cover any gaps between what they have and what they want.

Goals and Dreams

We like to start with your pie in the sky. Do you find yourself planning for your vacations more thoroughly than you do your retirement? A recent survey found one in five Americans spends more time planning our vacations than we spend planning our retirements.[18] Maybe it's because planning a vacation is less stressful: Having a week at the beach go awry is, well, a walk on the beach compared to running out of money in retirement. Whatever the case, perhaps it would be better if you thought of your retirement as a vacation in and of

---

[18] Malika Mitra. CNBC. August 2, 2019. "You're not alone if you spend more time planning your vacation than working on your finances." https://www.cnbc.com/2019/08/02/1-in-5-people-spend-more-time-planning-vacations-than-finances-survey.html

itself—no clocking in, no boss, no overtime. If you felt unlimited by financial strain, what would you do?

Would an endless vacation for you mean Paris and Rome? Would it mean mentoring at children's clubs or serving at the local soup kitchen? Or maybe it would mean deepening your ties to those immediately around you—neighbors, friends, and family. Maybe it would mean more time to take part in the hobbies and activities you love. Have you been considering a second (or even third) act as a small-business owner, turning a hobby or passion into a revenue source?

This is your time to daydream and answer the question: If you could do anything, what would you do?

After that, it's a matter of putting a dollar amount on it. What are the costs of round-the-world travel? One couple we know said their highest priority in retirement was being able to take each of their grandchildren on a cross-country vacation every year. That's a pretty specific goal—one that is reasonably easy to nail down a budget for.

Mr. and Mrs. Franz came in and told us they were eighteen months away from retirement. They even knew how many Mondays were between then and their retirement date. Mr. and Mrs. Franz knew exactly what they wanted to do the second they handed in their notice. They raised their two children just outside of Boston in the home they currently lived in, but told us they were going to sell it and move to Cape Cod in the summers and a condo in Florida in the winters. A series of dream vacations were even already planned out. On the itinerary were tours through Europe (Italy, France, Greece) and a relaxing getaway in the Caribbean. Because Mr. and Mrs. Franz were so specific with their post-retirement plans, we were able to successfully incorporate their vision of how retirement looked into the plan we created for them.

Current Budget

Compiling a current expense report is one of the trickiest pieces of retirement preparation. Many people assume the expenses of their lives in retirement will be different—lower. After all, there will be no drive to work, no need for a formal wardrobe, and, perhaps most impactful of all, no more saving for retirement!

Yet, we often underestimate our daily spending habits. That's why we typically ask our clients to bring in their bank statements for the past year—they are reflective of your *actual* spending, not just what you think you're spending.

Most people don't know how much they spend on a monthly basis and would most likely underestimate their expenses if they had to pick a figure. Many of us, however, know what we spend on an item-by-item basis. For example, we all know how much we spend on cable/internet, property taxes, utilities, etc. What's a little harder to estimate are items such as groceries and dining out, travel, maintenance and repairs, and gifts. We've developed a comprehensive budget analysis that makes it surprisingly easy to estimate how much income will be needed once retired. In addition to this number, we also recommend building in a "buffer" of 10 percent or more for miscellaneous items and expenses.

We can't count the number of times we have sat with a couple, asked them about their spending, and heard them throw out a number that seemed incredibly low. When we ask them where the number came from, they usually say they estimated based on their total bills. Yet, our spending is so much more than our mortgage, utilities, cable, phone, car, grocery, or credit card bills.

"What about clothes?" we ask, "Or dining out? What about gifts and coffees and last-minute birthday cards?" That's when the lights come on.

This is why we suggest collecting a year's worth of information. There is usually no such thing as a one-time purchase. Did you buy new furniture? Even if that is a rarity, do you think that will be the last time you *ever* buy furniture?

Another hefty expense is spending on the kids. Many of the couples we work with are quick to help their adult children, whether it's something like letting them live in the basement, paying for college, babysitting, paying an occasional bill, or contributing to a grandchild's college fund. They aren't alone—79 percent of Americans in 2018 said they had provided financial support for an adult child. And it's not unlikely for some parents to tap into their retirement funds to do so.[19]

Our clients sometimes protest that what they do for their grown children can stop in retirement. They don't *need* to help. But we get it. Parents like to feel needed. And, while you never want to neglect saving for retirement in favor of taking on financial risks (like your child's student debt), the parents who help their adult children do so in part because it helps them feel fulfilled.

When it comes down to expenses, including (and especially) spending on your family, don't make your initial calculations based on what you *could* whittle your budget down to if you *had* to. Instead, start from where you are. Who wants to live off a bare-bones bank account in retirement?

Other Expenses

Once you have nailed down your current budget and your dreams or goals for retirement, there are a few other outstanding pieces to think about—some expenses many people don't take the time to consider before making and executing a plan. But we're assuming you want to get it right, so let's take a look.

Housing

Do you know where you want to live in retirement? This makes up a substantial piece of your income puzzle—since the

---

[19] Lorie Konish. CNBC. October 2, 2018. "Parents Spend Twice as Much on Adult Children than They Save for Retirement."
https://www.cnbc.com/2018/10/02/parents-spend-twice-as-much-on-adult-children-than-saving-for-retirement.html

typical American household owns a home, and it's generally their largest asset—but it often goes unaccounted for until the last minute. [20]

Some people prefer to live right where they are for as long as they can. Others have been waiting for retirement to pull the trigger on an ambitious move, like purchasing a new house, or even downsizing. Whatever your plans and whatever your reasons, there are quite a few things to consider.

Mortgage

Do you still have a mortgage? What may have been a nice tax boon in your working years could turn into a financial burden in your retirement. After all, when you are on a limited income, a mortgage is just one more bill sapping your financial strength. It is something to put some thought into, whether you plan to age in place or are considering moving to your dream home, buying a house out of state, or living in a retirement community.

Upkeep and Taxes

A house without a mortgage still requires annual taxes. While it's tempting to think of this as a once-a-year expense, when you have limited earning potential, your annual tax bill might be something into which you should put a little more forethought.

The costs of homeownership aren't just monetary. When you find yourself dealing with more house than you need, it can drain your time and energy. From keeping clutter at bay to keeping the lawn mower running, upkeep can be extensive and expensive. For some, that's a challenge they heartily accept and can comfortably take on. For others, the idea of yard work or cleaning an area larger than they need feels foolish.

---

[20] Jann Swanson. Mortgage News Daily. August 28, 2019. "Homeownership is the Top Contributor to Household Wealth." http://www.mortgagenewsdaily.com/08282019_homeownership.asp

For instance, Peggy discovered after her knee replacement that most of her house was inaccessible to her when she was laid up.

"It felt ridiculous to pay someone else to dust and vacuum a house I was only living in 40 percent of!"

Practicality and Adaptability

Erik and Magda are looking to retire within the next two decades. They just sold their old three-bedroom ranch-style house. Their twins are in high school, and the couple has wanted to "upgrade" for years. Now they live in a gorgeous 1940s three-story house with all the kitchen space they ever wanted, five sprawling bedrooms, and a library and media room for themselves and their children. Within months of moving in, the couple realized a house perfect for their active teens would no longer be perfect for them in five to fifteen years.

"We are paying the mortgage for this house, but we've started saving for the next one," said Magda, "because who wants to climb two flights of stairs to their bedroom when they're seventy-eight?"

Others we know have encountered a similar situation in their personal lives. After a health crisis, one couple found the luxurious tub for two they toiled to install had become a specter of a bad slip and a potential safety risk. It's important to think through what your physical reality could be. We always emphasize to clients that they should plan for whatever their long-term future might hold, but it's amazing how many people don't give it much thought.

Contracts and Regulations

If you are looking into a cross-country move, be aware of new tax tables or local ordinances in the area where you are looking to move. After all, you don't want to experience sticker-shock when you are looking at downsizing or reducing your bills in retirement.

Along the same lines, if you are moving into a retirement community, be sure to look at the fine print. What happens if you must move into a different situation for long-term care? Will you be penalized? Will you be responsible for replacing your slot in the community? What are all the fees, and what do they cover?

Our typical experience, once we've built an income plan and incorporated a budget analysis, is clients have an excess of income compared to what they thought they would need.

Inflation

As we write this in 2020, America has experienced a long stretch of low inflation, with inflation not exceeding 4 percent since 1991.[21]

However, inflation isn't a one-time bump; it has a cumulative effect. Even with relatively low inflation over the past few decades, the $20 sneakers you bought your grade-schooler in 1991 will cost $37.90 to buy for your grandchild today.[22] What if, in retirement, we hit a stretch like the late '70s and early '80s, when annual inflation rates of 10 percent became the norm? It may be wise to consider some extra padding in your retirement income plan to account for any potential increase in inflation in the future.

Aging

Also, in the expense category, think about longevity. We all hope to age gracefully. However, it's important to face the prospect of aging with a sense of realism.

The elephant in the room for many families is long-term care: No one wants to admit they will likely need it, but

---

[21] US Inflation Calculator. January 2020. "Historical Inflation Rates." http://www.usinflationcalculator.com/inflation/historical-inflation-rates/
[22] Ibid.

estimates say as many as 70 percent of us will. [23] Aging is a significant piece of retirement income planning because you'll want to figure out how to set aside money for your care, either at home or away from it. The more comfortable you get with discussing your wishes and plans with your loved ones, the easier planning for the financial side of it can be.

We discuss health care and potential long-term care costs in more detail elsewhere in this book, but, suffice it to say, nursing home care is incredibly expensive and typically isn't something you get to choose when you will need.

It isn't just the costs of long-term care that pose a concern in living longer. It's also about covering the possible costs of everything else associated with living longer. For instance, if Henry retires from his job as a biochemical engineer at age sixty-five, perhaps he planned to have a very decent income for twenty years, until age eighty-five. But what if he lives until he's ninety-five? That's a whole third—ten years—more of personal income he will need.

Putting It All Together

Whew! So, you have pulled together what you have, and you have a pretty good idea of where you want to be. Now your financial professional and you can go about the work of arranging what assets you *have* to cover what you *need*—and how you might try to cover any gaps.

Like the proverbial man in the Bible who built his house on a rock, we like to help our clients figure out how to cover their day-to-day living expenses—their needs—with insurance and other guaranteed income sources like pensions and Social Security.

Everybody will have a different vision for what retirement will mean to them. For some, retirement means traveling the country or the world. For others, it's spending time with the

---

[23] Moll Law Group. 2019. "The Cost of Long-Term Care." https://www.molllawgroup.com/the-cost-of-long-term-care.html.

kids and grandkids. For even others, it's as simple as not having the day-to-day pressure of work and just relaxing.

The common denominator for most retirement plans, though, is income. We all need some level of income in order to fit the lifestyle we want to live. To this end, when we evaluate whether someone can retire how they see fit, we begin with an income roadmap. First, we evaluate existing guaranteed sources of income (including Social Security and/or pensions). Second, we look at their budget/expense analysis to determine how much income is needed. Next, we take an inventory of retirement assets (IRAs, 401(k)s, annuities, etc.) and look both at how much income these can reasonably and reliably produce while determining where risk/exposure to loss might be present.

Included in this analysis is incorporating the effect of estimated taxes on income; to hedge against future tax increases, we project retirement income going forward with a higher effective tax rate than what it would be under current tax brackets. When we put this plan together, we call it the "Generations Retirement Roadmap."

Again, you should keep in mind there isn't one single financial vehicle, asset, or source to fill all your needs, and that's okay. One of the challenges of planning for your income in retirement concerns figuring out what products and strategies to use. You can release some of that stress when you accept the fact you will probably need a diverse portfolio— potentially with bonds, stocks, insurance, and other income sources—not just one massive money pile.

One way to help shore up your income gaps is by working with your financial professional and a qualified tax advisor to mitigate your tax exposure. If you have a 401(k) or IRA, a tax advisor in your corner can help you figure out how and when to take distributions from your account in a way that doesn't push you into a higher tax bracket. Or you might learn how to use tax-advantaged bonds more effectively. Effective tax planning isn't necessarily about "adding" to your income. Especially regarding retirement, it's less about what you make than it is about what you keep. Paying a lower tax bill keeps more money in your pocket, which is where you want it when it comes to retirement income.

Now you can look at ways to cover your remaining retirement goals. Are there products like long-term care insurance specific to a certain kind of expense you anticipate? Is there a particular asset you want to use for your "play" money—money for trips and gifts for the grandkids? Is there any way you can portion off money for those charitable legacy plans?

Once you have analyzed your income wants, needs, and the assets to realistically cover them, you may have a gap. The masterstroke of a competent financial professional will be to help you figure out how you will cover that gap. Will you need to cut out a round of golf a week? Maybe skip the new car? Or will you need to take more substantial action?

One way to cover an income gap is to consider working longer or even part-time before retirement and even after that magical calendar date. This may not be the best "plan" for you; disabilities, work demands, and physical or emotional limitations can hinder the best-laid plans to continue working. However, if it is physically possible for you, this is one considerable way to help your assets last, for more than one reason.

In fact, about one in five Americans are still working past age sixty-five. This is a record percentage in the past half-century. While some do list their personal finances as a reason for staying on the job, others do so to avoid feeling bored in retirement, among other reasons.[24]

Because there are so many moving parts to creating a retirement plan, many people, including those who might in fact be well-positioned, don't have any idea as to where they

---

[24] Associated Press. October 9, 2018. "1 in 5 Americans over 65 are Still Waiting to Retire." https://nypost.com/2018/10/09/1-in-5-americans-over-65-are-still-waiting-to-retire/

really stand for retirement readiness. This is why we work with our clients in digestible, but meaningful, stages.

Even before looking at retirement accounts, we begin with a budget analysis. This is a great first step, and our budget process makes it simple. Once we start to project our income and compare that to the budget, many clients are pleased to see the result. Retirement can be a nebulous concept, but once people see it in black and white, i.e., monthly income versus expenses, it becomes more than just a concept.

When you're retired, you no longer have an employer paying you a steady check. It is up to you to make sure you have saved and planned for the income you need.

CHAPTER 5

Social Security

Social Security is often the foundation of retirement income. Backed by the strength of the U.S. Treasury, it provides perhaps the most dependable paycheck you will have in retirement.

From the time you collect your first paycheck from the job that made you a bonafide taxpayer (for Dave, it was packing bags at Shaw's in Randolph, Massachusetts, for $2.33 per hour—not bad for back then, since minimum wage was $1.89, so he was living the high life!), you are paying into the grand old Social Security system. What grew and developed out of the pressures of the Great Depression has become one of the most popular government programs in the country, and, if you pay in for the equivalent of ten years or more, you, too, can benefit from the Social Security program.

Now, before we get into the nitty-gritty of Social Security, we'd like to address a current concern: Will Social Security still be there for you when you reach retirement age?

The Future of Social Security

This question is ever-present as headlines trumpet an underfunded Social Security program, alongside the sea of baby boomers who are retiring in droves and the comparatively smaller pool of younger people who are bearing the responsibility of funding the system.

The Social Security Administration itself acknowledges this concern as each Social Security statement now bears an asterisk that continues near the end of the summary:

"*Your estimated benefits are based on current law. Congress has made changes to the law in the past and can do so at any time. The law governing benefit amounts may change because, by 2034, the payroll taxes collected will be enough to pay only about 79 percent of scheduled benefits."

Just a reminder, as if you needed one, that nothing in life is guaranteed.

Before you get too discouraged, though, here are a few thoughts to keep you going:

- Although those who retire after 2034 may only receive 79 cents on the dollar for their scheduled benefits, 79 percent is notably not zero.
- The Social Security Administration has made changes in the distant and near past to protect the fund's solvency, including increasing retirement ages and striking certain filing strategies.
- There are many changes Congress could make, and lawmakers are currently discussing how to fix the system, such as further increasing full retirement age and eligibility.
- One thing no one is seriously discussing? Reneging on current obligations to retirees or the soon-to-retire.

Take heart. The real answer to the question, "Will Social Security be there for me?" is still yes.

This question is an important one to consider when you look at how much we, as a nation, rely on this program. Did you know Social Security benefits replace about 40 percent of a person's original income when they retire?[25]

If you ask us, that's a pretty significant piece of your retirement income puzzle.

Another caveat? You may not realize this, but no one can legally "advise" you about your Social Security benefits.

"But, David and Matthew," you may be thinking, "isn't that part of what you do? And what about that nice gentleman at the Social Security Administration office I spoke with on the phone?"

Don't get us wrong. Social Security Administration employees know their stuff. They are trained to know policies and programs, and they are usually pretty quick to tell you what you can and cannot do. But the government specifically says, because Social Security is a benefit you alone have paid into and earned, your Social Security decisions, too, are yours alone.

When it comes to financial professionals, we can't push you in any directions, either, *but*—there's a big but here—working with a well-informed financial professional is still incredibly handy when it comes to your Social Security decisions. Why? Because someone who's worth his or her salt will know what withdrawal strategies might pertain to your specific situation and will ask questions that can help you determine what you are looking for when it comes to your Social Security.

For instance, some people want the highest possible monthly benefit. Others want to start their benefits early, not always because of financial need. We heard about one man who called in to start his Social Security payments the day he qualified, just because he liked to think of it as the government paying back a debt it owed him, and he enjoyed the feeling of receiving a check from Uncle Sam.

Whatever your reasons, questions, or feelings regarding Social Security, the decision is yours alone; but working with a

---

[25] Social Security Administration. "Learn About Social Security Programs." https://www.ssa.gov/planners/retire/r&m6.html

financial professional can help you put your options in perspective by showing you—both with industry knowledge and with proprietary software or planning processes— where your benefits fit into your overall strategy for retirement income.

One reason the federal government doesn't allow for "advice" related to Social Security, we suspect, is so no one can profit from giving you advice related to your Social Security benefit—or from providing any clarifications. Again, this is a sign of a good financial professional. Those who are passionate about their work will be knowledgeable about what benefit strategies might be to your advantage and will happily share those possible options with you.

Full Retirement Age

When it comes to Social Security, it seems like many people only think so far as "yes." They don't take the time to understand the various options available. Instead, because it is common knowledge you can begin your benefits at age sixty-two, that's what many of us do. While more people are opting to delay taking benefits, age sixty-two is still firmly the most popular age to start.[26]

What many people fail to understand is, by starting benefits early, they may be leaving a lot of money on the table. You see, the Social Security Administration bases your monthly benefit on two factors: your earnings history and your full retirement age (FRA).

From your earnings history, they pull the thirty-five years you made the most money and use a mathematical indexing formula to figure out a monthly average from those years. If

---

[26] Elizabeth O'Brien. Money. March 7, 2019. "This is the Age when Most People Claim Social Security—and When Experts Say You Really Should." http://money.com/money/5637694/this-is-the-age-when-most-people-claim-social-security-and-when-experts-say-you-really-should/

you paid into the system for less than thirty-five years, then every year you didn't pay in will be counted as a zero.

Once they have calculated what your monthly earning would be at FRA, the government then calculates what to put on your check based on how close you are to FRA. FRA was originally set at sixty-five, but, as the population aged and lifespans lengthened, the government shifted FRA later and later, based on an individual's year of birth. Check out the following chart to see when you will reach FRA.[27]

---

[27] Social Security Administration. "Full Retirement Age." https://www.ssa.gov/planners/retire/retirechart.html

Age to Receive Full Social Security Benefits*

(Called "full retirement age" [FRA] or "normal retirement age.")

Year of Birth*	FRA
1937 or earlier	65
1938	65 and 2 months
1939	65 and 4 months
1940	65 and 6 months
1941	65 and 8 months
1942	65 and 10 months
1943-1954	66
1955	66 and 2 months
1956	66 and 4 months
1957	66 and 6 months
1958	66 and 8 months
1959	66 and 10 months
1960 and later	67

If you were born on Jan. 1 of any year, you should refer to the previous year. (If you were born on the 1st of the month, we figure your benefit [and your full retirement age] as if your birthday was in the previous month.)

When you reach FRA, you are eligible to receive 100 percent of whatever the Social Security Administration says is your full monthly benefit.

Starting at age sixty-two, for every year before FRA you claim benefits, your monthly check is reduced by 5 percent or more. Conversely, for every year you delay taking benefits past FRA, your monthly benefit increases by 8 percent (until age seventy—after that, there is no monetary advantage to delaying Social Security benefits). While your circumstances and needs may vary, a lot of financial professionals still urge people to at least consider delaying until they reach age seventy.

Why Wait?[28]

Taking benefits early could affect your monthly check by _____.								
62	63	64	65	FRA 66	67	68	69	70
-25 %	-20 %	-13.3 %	-6.7 %	0	+8 %	+16 %	+24 %	+32 %

My Social Security

If you are over age thirty, you have probably received a notice from the Social Security Administration telling you to activate something called "My Social Security." This is a handy way to learn more about your particular benefit options, to keep track of what your earnings record looks like, and to calculate the benefits you have accrued over the years.

Essentially, My Social Security is an online account you can activate to see what your personal Social Security picture looks like, which you can do at www.ssa.gov/myaccount. This can be extremely helpful when it comes to planning for income in

[28] Social Security Administration. April 2019. "Can You Take Your Benefits Before Full Retirement Age?"
https://www.ssa.gov/planners/retire/applying2.html

retirement and figuring up the difference between your anticipated income versus anticipated expenses.

My Social Security is also helpful because it's a great way to see if there is a problem. For instance, we have heard of one woman who, through diligently checking her tax records against her Social Security profile, discovered her Social Security check was shortchanging her, based on her earnings history. After taking the discrepancy to the Social Security Administration, they sent her what they owed her in makeup benefits.

COLA

Social Security is a largely guaranteed piece of the retirement puzzle: If you get a statement that says to expect $1,000 a month, you can be sure you will receive $1,000 a month. But there is one variable detail, and that is something called the cost-of-living adjustment, or COLA.

The COLA is an increase in your monthly check meant to address inflation in everyday life. After all, your expenses will likely continue to experience inflation in retirement, but you will no longer have the opportunity for raises, bonuses, or promotions you had when you were working. Instead, Social Security receives an annual cost-of-living increase tied to the Department of Labor's Consumer Price Index for Urban Wage Earners and Clerical Workers, or CPI-W. If the CPI-W measurement shows inflation rose a certain amount for regular goods and services, then Social Security recipients will see that reflected in their COLA.

The COLA averages 4 percent, but in a no- or low-inflation environment, such as in 2010, 2011, and 2016, Social Security recipients will not receive an adjustment. Some view the COLA as a perk, bump, or bonus, but, in reality, it works more like this: Your mom sends you to the store with $2.50 for a gallon of milk. Milk costs exactly $2.50. The next week, you go back with that same amount, but it is now $2.52 for a gallon, so you go back to Mom, and she gives you 2 cents. You aren't bringing home more milk—it just costs more money.

So the COLA is less about "making more money" and more about keeping seniors' purchasing power from eroding when inflation is a big factor, such as in 1975, when it was 8 percent![29] Still, don't let that detract from your enthusiasm about COLAs; after all, what if Mom's solution was: "Here's the same $2.50; try to find pennies from somewhere else to get that milk!"?

Spousal Benefits

We've talked about FRA, but another big Social Security decision involves spousal benefits.

If you or your spouse has a long stretch of zeros in your earnings history—perhaps if one of you stayed home for years, caring for children or sick relatives—you may want to consider filing for spousal benefits instead of filing on your own earnings history. A spousal benefit can be up to 50 percent of the primary wage earner's benefit at full retirement age.

To begin drawing a spousal benefit, you must be at least sixty-two years old, and the primary wage earner must have already filed for his or her benefit. While there are penalties for taking spousal benefits early (you could lose up to 67.5 percent of your check for filing at age sixty-two), you cannot earn credits for delaying past full retirement age. [30]

As we said, the spousal benefit can be a big deal for those who don't have a very long pay history, but it's important to weigh your own earned benefits against the option of withdrawing based on a fraction of your spouse's benefits.

---

[29] Social Security Administration. "Cost-Of-Living Adjustment (COLA) Information for 2019." https://www.ssa.gov/cola/.
[30] Social Security Administration. "Retirement Planner: Benefits For You As A Spouse." https://www.ssa.gov/planners/retire/applying6.html

To look at how this could play out, let's use a hypothetical example of Mary Jane, who is sixty, and Peter, who is sixty-two.

Let's say Peter's benefit at FRA, in his case sixty-six, would be $1,600. If Peter begins his benefits right now, four years before FRA, his monthly check will be $1,200. If Mary Jane begins taking spousal benefits in two years at the earliest date possible, her monthly benefits will be reduced by 67.5 percent, to $520 per month (remember, at FRA, the most she can qualify for is half of Peter's FRA benefit).

What if Peter and Mary Jane both wait until FRA? At sixty-six, Peter begins taking his full benefit of $1,600 a month. Two years later, when she reaches age sixty-six, Mary Jane will qualify for $800 a month. By waiting until FRA, the couple's monthly benefit goes from $1,720 to $2,400.

What if Peter delays until age seventy to get his maximum possible benefit? For each year past FRA he delays, his monthly benefits increase by 8 percent. This means, at seventy, he could file for a monthly benefit of $2,112. However, delayed retirement credits do not affect spousal benefits, so as soon as Peter files at seventy, Mary Jane would also file (at age sixty-eight) for her maximum benefit of $800, so their highest possible combined monthly check is $2,912.[31]

When it comes to your Social Security benefits, you obviously will want to consider whether a monthly check based on a fraction of your spouse's earnings will be comparable to or larger than your own earnings history.

Divorced Spouses

There are a few considerations for those of us who have gone through a divorce. If you 1) were married for ten years or more *and* 2) have since been divorced for at least two years *and* 3)

---

[31] Office of the Chief Actuary. Social Security Administration. "Social Security Benefits: Benefits for Spouses."
https://www.ssa.gov/OACT/quickcalc/spouse.html#calculator

are unmarried *and* 4) your ex-spouse qualifies to begin Social Security, you qualify for a spousal benefit based on your ex-husband or ex-wife's earnings history at FRA. A divorced spousal benefit is different from the married spousal benefit in one way: You don't have to wait for your ex-spouse to file before you can file yourself.[32]

For instance, Charles and Moira were married for fifteen years before their divorce, when he was thirty-six and she was forty. Moira has been remarried for twenty years, and, although Charles briefly remarried, his second marriage ended after a few years. Charles' benefits are largely calculated based on his many years of volunteering in schools, meaning his personal monthly benefit is close to zero.

Although Moira has deferred her retirement, opting to delay benefits until she is seventy, Charles can begin taking benefits calculated from Moira's work history at FRA as early as sixty-two. However, he will also have the option of waiting until FRA to collect the maximum, or 50 percent of Moira's earned monthly benefit at her FRA.

Widowed Spouses

If your marriage ended with the death of your spouse, you might claim a benefit for your spouse's earned income as his or her widow/widower, called a survivor's benefit. Unlike a spousal benefit or divorced benefits, if your husband or wife dies, you can claim his or her full benefit. Also, unlike spousal benefits, if you need to, you can begin taking income when you turn sixty. However, as with other benefit options, your monthly check will be permanently reduced for withdrawing benefits before FRA.

If your spouse began taking benefits before he or she died, you can't delay withdrawing your survivor's benefits to get delayed credits; the Social Security Administration says you

---

[32] Social Security Administration. "Retirement Planner: If You Are Divorced." https://www.ssa.gov/planners/retire/divspouse.html

can only get as much from a survivor's benefit as your deceased spouse might have gotten, had he or she lived.[33]

Taxes, Taxes, Taxes

With Social Security, as with everything, it is important to consider taxes. It may be surprising, but your Social Security benefits are not tax-free. Despite having been taxed to accrue those benefits in the first place, you may have to pay Uncle Sam income taxes on up to 85 percent of your Social Security.

The Social Security Administration figures these taxes using what they call "the provisional income formula." Your provisional income formula differs from the adjusted gross income you use for your regular income taxes. Instead, to find out how much of your Social Security benefit is taxable, the Social Security Administration calculates it this way:

Provisional Income = Adjusted Gross Income + Nontaxable Interest + ½ of Social Security

See that piece about nontaxable interest? That generally means interest from government bonds and notes. It surprises many people that, although you may not pay taxes on those assets, their income will count against you when it comes to Social Security taxation.

Once you have figured out your provisional income (also called "combined income"), you can use the following chart to figure out your Social Security taxes.[34]

33 Social Security Administration. "Social Security Benefit Amounts For The Surviving Spouse By Year Of Birth." https://www.ssa.gov/planners/survivors/survivorchartred.html
34 Social Security Administration. "Benefits Planner: Income Taxes and Your Social Security Benefits." https://www.ssa.gov/planners/taxes.html

Taxes on Social Security		
Provisional Income = Adjusted Gross Income + Nontaxable Interest + ½ of Social Security		
If you are ____ and your provisional income is____, then...		Uncle Sam will tax ___ of your Social Security
Single	Married, filing jointly	
Less than $25,000	Less than $32,000	0%
$25,000 to $34,000	$32,000 to $44,000	Up to 50%
More than $34,000	More than $44,000	Up to 85%

This is one more reason it may benefit you to work with financial and tax professionals: They can look at your entire financial picture to make your overall retirement plan as tax-efficient as possible—including your Social Security benefit.

Here's an example of how we can help clients maximize their Social Security benefits while maximizing tax efficiency: We frequently see couples retiring around their full retirement age and who are planning on turning on their Social Security benefits immediately. But many of them also have IRA accounts or after-tax accounts and emergency savings.

Instead of turning on the Social Security benefits right away while beginning to withdraw from these other accounts, we often help them develop strategies for withdrawing from the after-tax accounts in a way that can save them thousands in taxes.

Working and Social Security: The Earnings Test

If you haven't reached FRA, but you started your Social Security benefits and are still working, things get a little hairy.

Because you have started Social Security payments, the Social Security Administration will pay out your benefits (at that reduced rate, of course, because you haven't reached your FRA). Yet, because you are working, the organization must also withhold from your check to add to your benefits, which you are already collecting. See how this complicates matters?

To straighten the situation, the government has what is called the earnings test. For 2020, you can earn up to $18,240 without it affecting your Social Security check. But, for every $2 you earn past that amount, the Social Security Administration will withhold $1. The earnings test loosens in the year of your FRA; if you are reaching FRA in 2020, you can earn up to $48,600 before you run into the earnings test, and the government only withholds $1 for every $3 past that amount. The month you reach FRA, you are no longer subject to any earnings withholding. For instance, if you are still working and will turn sixty-six on December 28, 2020, you would only have to worry about the earnings test until December, and then you can ignore it entirely. Keep in mind, the money the government withholds from your Social Security benefits while you are working before FRA will be tacked back onto your benefits check after FRA.[35]

Because of our philosophy that income is the first part of a retirement plan, it's crucial to optimize Social Security, since it plays a major part in most people's income in retirement.

---

[35] Social Security Administration. "Exempt Amounts Under the Earnings Test." https://www.ssa.gov/oact/cola/rtea.html

CHAPTER 6

401(k)s & IRAs

Have you heard? Today's retirement is not your parents' retirement. You see, back in the day, it was pretty common to work for one company for the vast majority of your career and then retire with a gold watch and a pension.

The gold watch was a symbol of the quality time you had put in at that company, but the pension was more than a symbol. Instead, it was a guarantee—as solid as your employer—that they would repay your hard work with a certain amount of income in your old age. Did you see the caveat there? Your pension's guarantee was *as solid as your employer.* The problem was, what if your employer went under?

Companies that failed couldn't pay their retired employees' pensions, leading to financial challenges for many. Beginning in 1974 with Congress' passage of the Employee Retirement Income Security Act, federal legislation and regulations aimed at protecting retirees were everywhere. One piece of legislation included a relatively obscure section of the Internal Revenue Code, added in 1978. Section 401(k), to be specific.

IRC section 401, subsection k, created tax advantages for employer-sponsored financial products, even if the main contributor was the employee him or herself. Over the years, more employers took note, beginning an age of transition away from pensions and toward 401(k) plans. A 401(k) is a retirement account with certain tax benefits and restrictions on the investments or other financial products inside of it.

Essentially, 401(k)s and their individual retirement account (IRA) counterparts are "wrappers" that provide tax benefits around assets; typically, the assets that compose IRAs and 401(k)s are mutual funds, stock and bond mixes, and money market accounts. However, IRA and 401(k) contents are becoming more diverse these days, with some companies offering different kinds of annuity options within their plans.

Where pensions are defined-*benefit* plans, 401(k)s and IRAs are defined-*contribution* plans. The one-word change outlines the basic difference. Pensions spell out what you can expect to receive from the plan but not necessarily how much money it will take to fund those benefits. With 401(k)s, an employer sets a standard for how much they will contribute (if any), and you can be certain of what you are contributing. Still, there is no outline for what you can expect to receive in return for those contributions.

Modern employment looks very different. A 2018 survey by the Bureau of Labor Statistics determined U.S. workers stayed with their employers a median of about four years. Workers ages fifty-five to sixty-four had a little more staying power and were most likely to stay with their employer for about ten years.[36] Additionally, the outlook on the benefits front is different today, too. In 1979, 38 percent of workers had pensions. But 401(k)s are rising in number, with about 55 million American workers enrolled in a plan.[37]

A far cry from a pension and gold watch, wouldn't you say?

For the lucky few among us who still have a pension, it opens up options. Of course, you could start an income stream from the pension, but many plans have more flexibility built in

---

[36] Bureau of Labor Statistics. September 20,2018. "Employee Tenure Summary." https://www.bls.gov/news.release/tenure.nr0.htm

[37] Investment Company Institute. December 31, 2018. "Frequently Asked Questions about 401(k) Plan Research." https://www.ici.org/policy/retirement/plan/401k/faqs_401k

than just that. Some pensions allow rollovers into an IRA, allowing the principal to be invested as you see fit. Many clients, especially ones who are married or who have children, are worried about what would happen if they pass away sooner rather than later. Using a rollover, the principal of the pension plan can be structured to meet customized goals, such as passing on a legacy, instead of the "take it or leave it" standard options of most plans.

If there is anything to learn from this paradigm shift, it's that you must look out for yourself. Whether you have worked for a company for two years or twenty, you are still the one who has to look out for your own best interests. That holds doubly true when it comes to preparing for retirement. If you are one of the lucky ones who still has a pension, good for you. But for the rest of us, it is likely a 401(k)—or possibly one of its nonprofit- or government-sector counterparts, a 403(b) or 457 plan—is one of your biggest assets for retirement.

Some employers offer incentives to contribute to their company plans, like a company match. On that subject, we have one thing to say: *Do it!* Nothing in life is free, as they say, but a company match on your retirement funds is about as close to free money as it gets. If you can make the minimum to qualify for your company's match at all, go for it.

Now, it's likely, during our working years, we mostly "set and forget" our 401(k) funding. Because it is tax-advantaged, your employer is taking money from your paycheck—before taxes—and putting it into your plan for you. Maybe you got to pick a selection of investments, or maybe your company only offers one choice of investment in your 401(k). Either way, while you are gainfully employed, your most impactful decision may just be the decision to continue funding your plan in the first place. But, when you are ready to retire or move jobs, you have choices to make requiring a little more thought and care.

When you are ready to part ways with your job, you have a few options:

- Leave the money where it is

- Take the cash (and pay income taxes and perhaps a 10 percent additional federal tax if you are younger than age fifty-nine-and-one-half)
- Transfer the money to another employer plan (if the new plan allows)
- Roll the money over into a self-directed IRA

Now, these are just general options. You will have to decide, hopefully with the help of a financial professional, what's right for you. For instance, 401(k)s are typically pretty closely tied to the companies offering them, so when changing jobs, it may not always be possible to transfer a 401(k) to another 401(k). Leaving the money where it is may also be out of the question—some companies have direct cash payout or rollover policies once someone is no longer employed.

Also, remember what we said earlier about how we change jobs more often these days? That means you likely have a 401(k) with your current company, but you may also have a string of retirement accounts trailing you from other jobs.

In our retirement seminars, we discuss the concept of a junk drawer. Everybody has a junk drawer . . . you might be picturing yours right now. There might be some old pens, gum, a calculator, maybe batteries from ten years ago . . . etc. Regardless, we all have a junk drawer, and most of us say we'll organize it someday, but not today.

In reality, an unorganized junk drawer doesn't have an adverse impact on our lives in any meaningful way. But we relate this to a "financial junk drawer" that many of us have. What do we mean by "financial junk drawer"? Well, if you're like most people, you might have a 401(k) at your current job, an IRA or two or three at different brokerage companies or advisors, or an old 401(k) or pension plan that you just never got to rolling over from an old job you left long ago. Unlike the junk drawers in our kitchens, the "financial junk drawer" needs to be organized sooner rather than later. If everything's spread out, it's easy to feel overwhelmed and next to impossible to have a coherent strategy. That's why we urge our seminar attendees to consider consolidating accounts and to begin to think about developing a strategy that addresses their retirement goals.

When it comes to your retirement income, it's important to be able to pull together *all* your assets, so you can examine what you have and where, and then decide what you will do with it.

Tax-Qualified, Tax-Preferred, Tax-Deferred ... Still TAXED

Financial media often cite IRAs and 401(k)s for their tax benefits. After all, with traditional plans, you put your money in, pre-tax, and it hopefully grows for years, even decades, untaxed. That's why these accounts are called "tax-qualified" or "tax-deferred" assets. They aren't *tax-free!* Rarely does Uncle Sam allow business to continue without receiving his piece of the pie, and your retirement assets are no different. If you didn't pay taxes on the front end, you will pay taxes on the money you withdraw from these accounts in retirement. Don't get us wrong: This isn't an inherently good or bad thing; it's just the way it is. It's important to understand, though, for the sake of planning ahead.

In retirement, many people assume they will be in a lower tax bracket. Are you planning to pare down your lifestyle in retirement? Perhaps you are, and perhaps you will have substantially less income in retirement. But many of our clients tell us they want to live life more or less the same as they always have. The money they would previously have spent on business attire or gas for their commute they now want to spend on hobbies and grandchildren. That's all fine, and for many of them, it is doable, but does it put them in a lower tax bracket? Probably not.

Keep in mind, IRAs, 401(k)s, and their alternatives have a few limitations because of their special tax status. For one thing, the IRS sets limits on your contributions to these retirement accounts. If you are contributing to a 401(k) or an equivalent nonprofit or government plan, your annual contribution limit is $19,500 (as of 2020). If you are fifty or older, the IRS allows additional contributions, called "catch-up contributions," of up to $6,500 on top of the regular limit of $19,500. For an IRA, the limit is $6,000, with a catch-up limit of an additional $1,000. [38]

Because their tax advantages come from their intended use as retirement income, withdrawing funds from these accounts before you turn fifty-nine-and-one-half can carry stiff penalties. In addition to fees your investment management company might charge, you will have to pay income tax *and* a 10 percent federal tax penalty, with few exceptions.

The fifty-nine-and-one-half rule for retirement accounts is incredibly important to remember, especially when you're young. Younger workers are often tempted to cash out an IRA from a previous employer and then are surprised to find their checks missing 20 percent of the account value to income taxes, penalty taxes, and account fees.

Many millennials we see in our practice say, while they may be socking money away in their workplace retirement plan, it is often the *only* place they are saving. This could be problematic later because of the fifty-nine-and-one-half rule; what if you have an emergency? It is important to fund your retirement, but you need to have some liquid assets handy as emergency funds. This can help you avoid breaking into your retirement accounts and incurring taxes and penalties because of the fifty-nine-and-one-half rule.

---

[38] Troy Segal. Investopedia. January 17,2020. "What Are the Roth 401(k) Contribution Limits?"
https://www.investopedia.com/ask/answers/102714/what-are-roth-401k-contibution-limits.asp

RMDs

Remember how we talked about the 401(k) or IRA being a "tax wrapper" for your funds? Well, eventually, Uncle Sam will want a bite of that candy bar. So, when you turn seventy-two, the government requires you withdraw a portion of your account, which the IRS calculates based on the size of your account and your estimated lifespan. This required minimum distribution, or RMD, is the government's insurance it will collect some taxes, at some point, from your earnings. Because you didn't pay taxes on the front end, you will now pay income taxes on whatever you withdraw, including your RMDs. Also, let us just remind you not to play chicken with the U.S. government; if you don't take your RMDs starting at seventy-two, you will have to write a check to the IRS for *50 percent* of the amount of your missed RMDs.

If you don't need income from your retirement accounts, RMDs can seem like more of a tax burden than an income boon. While some people prefer to reinvest their RMDs, this comes with the possibility of additional taxation: You'll pay income taxes on your RMDs and then capital gains taxes on the growth of your investments. If you are legacy minded, there are other ways to use RMDs, many of which have tax benefits.

Permanent Life Insurance
One way to turn those pesky RMDs into a legacy is through permanent life insurance. Assuming you need the death benefit coverage and can qualify for it medically, if properly structured, these products can pass on a sizeable death benefit to your beneficiaries, tax-free, as part of your general legacy plan.

ILIT
Another way to use RMDs toward your legacy is to work with an estate planning attorney to create an irrevocable life

insurance trust (ILIT). This is basically a permanent life insurance policy placed within a trust. Because the trust is irrevocable, you would relinquish control of it, but, unlike with just a permanent life insurance policy, your death benefit won't count toward your taxable estate.

Annuities

Because annuities can be tax-deferred, using all or a portion of your RMDs to fund an annuity contract can be one way to further delay taxation while guaranteeing your income payments (either to you or your loved ones) later. (Assuming you don't need the income from the RMDs during your retirement.)

Qualified Charitable Distributions

If you are charity-minded, you may use your RMDs toward a charitable organization instead of using them for income. You must do this directly from your retirement account (you can't take the RMD check and *then* pay the charity) for your withdrawals to be qualified charitable distributions (QCDs), but this is one way of realizing some of the benefits of a charitable legacy during your own lifetime. You will not need to pay taxes on your QCDs, and they won't count toward your annual charitable tax deduction limit, plus you'll be able to see how the organization you are supporting uses your donations. You should consult a financial professional on how to correctly make a QCD, particularly since the SECURE Act of 2019 has implemented a few regulations on this point.[39]

---

[39] Bob Carlson. Forbes. January 28, 2020. "More Questions And Answers About The SECURE Act."
https://www.forbes.com/sites/bobcarlson/2020/01/28/more-questions-and-answers-about-the-secure-act/#113d49564869

Roth IRA

Since the Taxpayer Relief Act of 1997, there has been a different kind of retirement account, or "tax wrapper," available to the public: the Roth. Roth IRAs and Roth 401(k)s each differ from their traditional counterparts in one big way: You pay your taxes on the front end. This means, once your post-tax money is in the Roth account, as long as you follow the rules and limitations of that account (take withdrawals after age fifty-nine-and-one-half and the account has been open for at least five years), your distributions are truly tax-free. You won't pay income tax when you take withdrawals, so, in turn, you don't have to worry about RMDs. However, Roth accounts have the same limitations as traditional 401(k)s and IRAs when it comes to withdrawing money before age fifty-nine-and-one-half.

Under certain circumstances, we might recommend converting from a traditional IRA to a Roth IRA. Although these are not hard and fast rules, here's a good, typical candidate for a Roth conversion: 1) Someone who's younger and who won't need to take distributions from the Roth IRA for at least ten years (typically mid-fifties and earlier). 2) Clients who might have substantial RMD issues down the line if their traditional IRA balances are much in excess of what would be needed to support lifestyle/income. 3) Someone who has enough money in non-taxable assets on the side to pay the taxes resulting from the conversion. It defeats the purpose of the conversion to pay the taxes out of the principal of the converted IRA.

Taking Charge

As mentioned earlier, the 401(k) and IRA have largely replaced pensions, but they aren't an equal trade.

Pensions are employer-funded; the money feeding into them is money that wouldn't ever show up on your pay stub.

Because 401(k)s are self-funded, you must actively and consciously save. This distinction has made a difference when it comes to funding retirement. According to one NerdWallet article, the average 401(k) balance for a person age sixty to sixty-nine is $198,600, but the median likely tells the full story. The median 401(k) balance for a person age sixty to sixty-nine is $63,000. The article also cites the general suggestion to aim, by age thirty, to have saved up an amount equal to 50 percent to 100 percent of your annual salary.[40] For some thirty-year-olds, saving half an annual salary by age thirty is more than some sixty-to-sixty-nine-year-olds have saved for their entire lives

There can be many reasons why people underfund their retirement plans, like being overwhelmed by the investment choices or taking withdrawals from IRAs when they leave an employer, but the reason at the top of the list is this: People simply aren't participating to begin with.

So, whether you use a 401(k) with an employer or an IRA alternative with a private company, separate from your workplace, the most important retirement savings decision you can make is to sock away your money somewhere in the first place.

---

[40] Arielle O'Shea. Nerd Wallet. January 24, 2019. "The Average 401(k) Balance by Age." https://www.nerdwallet.com/article/investing/the-average-401k-balance-by-age

CHAPTER 7

Annuities

In our practice, we offer our clients a variety of products—
from securities to insurance—all designed to help them
reach their financial goals. You may be wondering: Why
single out a single product in this book?

Well, while most of our clients have a pretty good
understanding of business and finance, we sometimes find
those who have the impression there must be magic involved.
Some people assume there is a finance wand we can wave to
change years' worth of savings into a strategy for retirement
income. But it's not as easy as a goose laying golden eggs or
the Fairy Godmother turning a pumpkin into a coach!

Finances aren't magic; it takes lots of hard work and,
typically, several financial products and strategies to pull
together a complete retirement plan. Of all the financial
products we work with, it seems people find none more
mysterious than annuities. And, if we may say, even some of
those who recognize the word "annuity" have a limited
understanding of the product. So, in the interest of
demystifying annuities, let us tell you a little about what an
annuity is.

In general, insurance is a financial hedge against risk. Car
owners buy auto insurance to protect their finances in case
they injure someone or someone injures them. Homeowners
have house insurance to protect their finances in case of a fire,

flood, or another disaster. People have life insurance to protect their finances in case of untimely death. Almost juxtaposed to life insurance, people have annuities in case of a long life; annuities can give you financial protection by providing consistent and reliable income payments.

The basic premise of an annuity is you, the annuitant, pay an insurance company some amount in exchange for their contractual guarantee they will pay you income for a certain time period. How that company pays you, for how long, and how much they offer are all determined by the annuity contract you enter into with the insurance company.

How You Get Paid

There are two ways for an annuity contract to provide income: The first is through what is called annuitization, and the second is through the use of income riders. We'll get into income riders in a bit, but let's talk about annuitization. That nice, long word is, in our opinion, one reason annuities have a reputation for mystery and misinformation.

Annuitization

When someone "annuitizes" a contract, it is the point where he or she turns on the income stream. Once a contract has been annuitized, there is no going back. With annuities, if the policyholder lives longer than the insurance company planned, the insurance company is still obligated to pay him or her, even if the payments end up being way more than the contract's actual value. If, however, the policyholder dies an untimely death, depending on the contract type, the insurance company may keep anything left of the money that funded the annuity—nothing would be paid out to the contract holder's survivors. You see where that could make some people balk?

At a high level, here's how it looks from the insurance company's side: Imagine the company has a "pie" of ten people, who all buy contracts at the same time. In the beginning, ten people receive income paid out by the company. A few, let's say three, die earlier on. As others age, they too die, many of them breaking even, with their pieces of the pie reaching zero around the time they pass away. One or two people even live well past the others, and, by the time they pass away, they have long since hit zero on the values of their contracts.

Now, we use this pie illustration as a way to show you the original concept of annuitization and how it works, from the perspectives of both an insurer and a contract holder. It's important to note that insurance companies don't rely solely on individuals passing away to pay other income to others, however. Insurance companies invest the premiums they collect from annuity owners and use the investment earnings to help pay income to their customers. Modern annuities have so many bells and whistles the picture we just described seems too simplified to do them justice, but it's important to at least have a basic concept of annuitization.

Riders

Speaking of bells and whistles, let's talk about riders. Modern annuities have a lot of different options these days, many in the form of riders you can add to your contract for a fee—usually about 1 percent of the contract value per year. Each rider has its particulars, and the types of riders available will vary by the type of annuity contract purchased, but we'll just briefly outline some of these little extras:

- Lifetime income rider: Contract guarantees you an enhanced income for life
- Death benefit rider: Contract pays an enhanced death benefit to your beneficiaries even if you have annuitized
- Return of premium rider: Guarantees you (or your beneficiaries) will at least receive back the premium value of the annuity

- Long-term care rider: Provides a certain amount, sometimes as much as twice the principal value of the contract, to help pay for long-term care if the contract holder is moved to a nursing home or assisted living situation

This isn't an extensive look, and usually the riders have fancier names based on the issuing company, like "Lorem Ipsum Insurance Company Income Preferred Bonus Fixed Index Annuity rider," but we just wanted to show you what some of the general options are in layperson's terms.

Types of Annuities

Annuities break down into four basic types: immediate, variable, fixed, and fixed index.

Immediate

Immediate annuities primarily rely on annuitization to provide income—you give the insurance company a lump sum up front, and your payments begin immediately. Once you begin receiving income payments, the transaction is irreversible, and you no longer have access to your money in a lump sum. When you die, any remaining contract value is typically forfeited to the insurance company.

All other annuity contract types are "deferred" contracts, meaning you fund your policy as a lump sum or over a period of years and you give it the opportunity to grow over time—sometimes years, sometimes decades.

Variable

A variable annuity is an insurance contract as well as an investment. It's sold by insurance companies, but only through someone who is registered to sell investment products. With a variable annuity contract, the insurance company pools the premiums from annuity holders and invests in subaccounts that are tied to the stock market.

This makes it a bit different from the other annuity contract types because it is the only contract where your money is subject to losses because of market declines. Your contract value has a greater opportunity to grow, but it also stands to lose. Additionally, your contract's value will be subject to the underlying investment's fees and limitations—including capital gains taxes, management fees, etc. Once it is time for you to receive income from the contract, the insurance company will pay you a certain income, locked in at whatever your contract's value was.

Variable annuities can sometimes give other types of annuities a bad name. Here's why: One, they tend to have high expenses. By the time contract fees, mortality expenses, rider charges, fund fees, and other expenses are factored in, we typically see variable annuities reach the 3-4 percent expense level annually. A $250,000 variable annuity with 4 percent annual expenses would cost the client $10,000 per year in fees! Ouch! Second, they can tend to be complex instruments with many moving parts. Sometimes they are discussed and purchased for some guarantee, but many clients are surprised to find out there are fewer guarantees in these than originally believed. In fact, the principal of the account, assuming it's invested in market-linked sub-accounts, is not guaranteed and is subject to loss. That's why we stay away from recommending variable annuities to clients who need protection of their principal. If clients want guaranteed principal and income, we look to different types of annuities to accomplish that goal.

Fixed

A traditional fixed annuity is pretty straightforward. You purchase a contract with a guaranteed interest rate and, when you are ready, the insurance company will make regular income payments to you at whatever payout rate your contract guarantees. Those payments will continue for the rest of your life and, if you choose, for the remainder of your spouse's life.

Fixed annuities don't have much in the way of upside potential, but many people like them for their guarantees (after all, if your Aunt May lives to be ninety-five, knowing she has a paycheck later in life can be her mental and financial safety net), as well as for their predictability. Unlike variable annuities, which are subject to market risk and might be up one year and down the next, you can easily calculate the value of your fixed annuity over your lifetime.

Fixed Index

To recap, variable annuities take on more risk to offer more possibilities to grow. Fixed annuities have less potential growth, but they protect your principal. In the last couple of decades, many insurance companies have retooled their product line to offer fixed index annuities, which are sort of midway between variable and fixed annuities on that risk/reward spectrum. Fixed index annuities offer greater growth potential than traditional fixed annuities but less than variable annuities. Like traditional fixed annuities, however, fixed index annuities are protected from downside market losses.

Fixed index annuities earn interest that is tied to the market, meaning that, instead of your contract value growing at a set interest rate like a traditional fixed annuity, it has the potential to grow within a range. Your contract's value is credited interest based on the performance of an external market index like the S&P 500 while never being invested in the market itself. You can't invest in the S&P 500 directly, but each year, your annuity has the potential to earn interest based on the chosen index's performance, submit to limits set by the company such as caps, spreads and participation rates. For instance, if your contract caps your interest at 5 percent, then in a year that the S&P 500 gains 3 percent, your annuity value increases 3 percent. If the S&P 500 gains 35 percent, your annuity value gets a 5 percent interest bump. But since your money isn't actually invested in the market with a fixed index annuity, if the market nosedives (such as happened during 2000, 2008 and 2020, anyone?) you won't see any increase in your contract value. Conversely, there will also be no decrease in your contract value—no matter how badly the market performed, as long as you follow the terms of the contract, you won't lose any of the interest you were credited in previous years.

So, what if the S&P 500 shows a market loss of 30 percent? Your contract value isn't going anywhere (unless you purchased an optional rider—this charge will still come out of your annuity value each year). For those who are more interested in protection than growth potential, fixed index annuities can be an attractive option because, when the stock market has a long period of positive performance, a fixed index annuity can enjoy conservative growth, even potentially offsetting the effects of inflation. And, during stretches where the stock market is erratic and stock values across the board take significant losses? Fixed index annuities won't lose anything due to the stock market volatility.

There are two main reasons why many pre-retirees and retirees alike might take a look at FIAs. First, they offer the opportunity to earn reasonable interest rates without the risk of loss of principal.

Second, some FIAs have additional/optional features, called "riders," that could fit the particular need of a client. The most common type of rider we recommend to clients is an income rider, which typically guarantees a lifetime stream of income as long as the client, and possibly their spouse, lives. This rider maintains the ability to access principal of the account if needed, and it allows the holder to pass on the balance of the account to beneficiaries if the client happens to pass before the money runs out. In the case of longevity, however, these income riders can help reduce the fear of running out of income, since, if the account balance ever runs out, the insurance company will still keep sending income checks as long as the client or one spouse is still alive.

Other Things to Know About Annuities

We just talked about the four kinds of annuity contracts available, but all of them have some commonalities as annuities.

For all annuities, the contractual guarantees are only as strong as the insurance company that sells the product, which makes it important to thoroughly check the credit ratings of any company whose products you are considering.

Annuities are tax-deferred, meaning you don't have to pay taxes on interest earnings each year as the contract value grows. Instead, you will pay ordinary income taxes on your withdrawals. These are meant to be long-term products, so, like other tax-advantaged products, if you begin taking withdrawals from your contract before age fifty-nine-and-one-half, you may also have to pay a 10 percent federal tax penalty. Also, while annuities are generally considered illiquid, most contracts allow you to withdraw up to 10 percent of your contract value every year. Withdraw more, however, and you could incur additional surrender penalties.

Keep in mind, your withdrawals will deplete the accumulated cash value, death benefit, and, possibly, the rider values of your contract.

Along the lines of what we just discussed, annuities have two main uses in our clients' portfolios. One is for clients who want to still grow their money but not have to take on any market risk. The other is they have a fit for clients who want to have guaranteed income they or their spouse can never outlive, even if the balance of the account goes to zero. Often times, people like using annuities to supplement Social Security and pension income if these sources don't provide enough to cover basic or lifestyle expenses. Because most clients are reassured these income payments will not have to be adjusted downward, they have the potential to supplement from market-based products if there is a downturn. For clients who want a level of certainty and predictability, annuities can offer this.

Annuities aren't for everyone, but it's important to understand them before saying "yea" or "nay" on whether they fit into your plan; otherwise, you're not operating with complete information, wouldn't you agree? Regardless, you should talk to a financial professional who can help you understand annuities, help you dissect your particular financial needs, and help show you whether an annuity is appropriate for your retirement income plan.

CHAPTER 8

Estate & Legacy

I n our practice, we devote a significant portion of our time to matters of estates. That doesn't mean drawing up wills or trusts or putting together powers of attorney or anything like that. After all, we're not estate planning attorneys. But we are financial professionals, and what part of the "estate" isn't affected by money matters?

We've included this chapter because we have seen many people do estate planning wrong. Clients, or clients' families, have come in after experiencing a death in the family and have found themselves in the middle of probate, high taxes, or a discovery of something unforeseen (often long-term care) draining the estate.

We have also seen people do estate planning right: clients or families who visit our office to talk about legacies and how to make them last and adult children who have room to grieve without an added burden of unintended costs, without stress from a family ruptured because of inadequate planning.

We'll share some of these stories here. However, We're not going to give you specific advice, since everyone's situation is unique. We only want to give you some things to think about and to underscore the importance of planning ahead.

Having an estate plan is not just about dying. There are many important pieces to the puzzle such as trusts, powers of attorney, and health care proxies that have as much to do with what happens during your life as it does afterward.

In this context, most clients recognize the need to update or create some basic documents to cover their bases once the retirement income and investment plan is taken care of. For clients who want to get these done, we have a strategic partnership with an estate planning attorney who specializes in this field. Having this attorney in house allows us to help clients seamlessly integrate their financial and legal plans.

You Can't Take It With You

When it comes to legacy and estate planning, the most important thing is to *do it*. We have heard people from clients to celebrities (rap artist Snoop Dogg comes to mind) say they aren't interested in what happens to their assets when they die because they'll be dead. That's certainly one way to look at it. But we think that's a very selfish way to go about things—we all have people and causes we care about, and those who care about us. Even if the people we love don't *need* what we leave behind, they can still be fined or legally tied up in the probate process or burial costs if we don't plan for those. And that's not even considering what happens if you become incapacitated at some point while you are still alive. Having a plan in place can greatly reduce the stress of responsibilities for your loved ones; it's just a loving thing to do.

Documents

There are a few documents that lay the groundwork of legacy planning. You've probably heard of all or most of them, but we'd like to review what they are and how people commonly use them. These are all things you should talk about with an estate planning attorney to establish your legacy.

Powers of Attorney

A power of attorney, or POA, is a document giving someone the authority to act on your behalf and in your best interests. These come in handy in situations where you cannot be present (think a vacation where you get stuck in Canada) or, for durable powers of attorney, even when you are incapacitated (think in a coma or coping with dementia).

It is important to have powers of attorney in place and to appoint someone you trust to act on your behalf in these matters. Have you ever heard of someone who was incapacitated after a car accident, whether from head trauma or being in a coma for weeks—sometimes months? Do you think their bills stopped coming due during that time? We like our phone company and our bank, but neither one is about to put a moratorium on sending us bills, particularly not for an extended or interminable period. A power of attorney would have the authority to pay your mortgage or cancel your cable while you are unable.

You can have multiple POAs and require them to act jointly.
What this looks like: Do you think two heads are better than one? One man, Chris, significantly relied on his two sons' opinions for both his business and personal matters. He appointed both sons as joint POA, requiring both their signoffs for his medical and financial matters.

You can have multiple POAs who can act independently.
What this looks like: Irene had three children with whom she routinely stayed. They lived in different areas of the country, which she thought was an advantage; one month she might be hiking out West, the next she could enjoy the newest off-Broadway production, and the next she could soak up some Southern sun. She named her three children as independently

authorized POAs, so, if something happened, no matter where she was, the child closest could step in to act on her behalf.

You can have POAs who have different responsibilities.

What this looks like: Although Luke's friend Claire, a nurse, was his go-to and POA for health-related issues, financial matters usually made her nervous, so he appointed his good neighbor, Matt, as his POA in all of his financial and legal matters.

In addition to POAs, it may be helpful to have an advanced medical directive. This is a document where you have pre-decided what choices you would make about different health scenarios. An advanced medical directive can help ease the burden for your medical POA and loved ones, particularly when it comes to end-of-life care.

Over the course of many years, we've had many instances where clients have unfortunately been incapacitated. Because of the planning that integrated their financial and legal plan, they were able to have their designated POA or HCP make the right choices for them. Without planning, the family would have had to go to court and spend time and money during a time of extreme stress. Luckily, families and clients who have planned are able to avoid an extra burden of time and cost when their loved ones need them most.

Wills

Perhaps the most basic document of legacy planning, a will is a legal document wherein you outline your wishes for your estate. When it comes to your estate after your death, having a will is the foundation of your legacy. Without one, your loved ones are left behind, guessing what you would have wanted, and the court will likely split your assets according to the state's defaults. Maybe that's exactly what you wanted, as far as anyone knows, right? Because even if you told your nephew he could have your car he's been driving, if it's not in writing, it still might go to the brother, sister, son, or daughter to whom you aren't speaking.

However, it may not be enough just to have a will. Even with a will, your assets will be subject to probate. Probate is what we call the state's process for determining a will's validity. A judge will go through your will to question if it conflicts with state law, if it is the most up-to-date document, if you were mentally competent at the time it was in order, etc. For some, this is a quick, easily-resolved process. For others, particularly if someone steps forward to contest the will, it may take years to settle, all the while subjecting the assets to court costs and attorney's fees.

One other undesirable piece of the probate process is that it is a public process. That means anyone can go to the courthouse, ask for copies of the case, and discover your assets. They can also see who is slated to receive what and who is disputing.

A couple years ago we had two sisters come to us after losing their mom. As traumatic as losing their mom was for them, they had to deal with a completely undesirable situation. Their estranged brother, who had a history of financial and legal issues, decided to challenge the passing of assets to the sisters. While the mom had no intention of leaving him any assets, she never bothered to do any planning. This cost the sisters tens of thousands of dollars in lawyer's fees and was only resolved three months ago. The failure of the mom to do any planning made it nearly impossible for her children to wrap up the financial aftermath of her passing for nearly two years. We're sure that if anyone had asked her while she was still living to commit to paper what she would have wanted in a formal estate plan, this situation certainly would have been avoidable.

It's also important to remember beneficiary lines trump wills. So, that large life insurance policy? What if, when you bought it fifteen years ago, you wrote your ex-husband's name on the beneficiary line? Even if you stipulate otherwise in your will, the company that holds your policy will pay out to your ex-spouse. Or, how about the thousands of dollars in your IRA you dedicated to the children thirty years ago, but one of your children was killed in a car accident, leaving his wife and two toddlers behind? That IRA is going to transfer to your remaining children, with nothing for your daughter-in-law and grandchildren.

That may paint a grim portrait, but we can't underscore enough the importance of working with a skilled estate planning attorney to keep your will and beneficiary lines up to date as your life changes, for the sake of your loved ones.

One nearly disastrous example of not updating beneficiaries occurred last year when a client came into our office. She had been at her job for over thirty years, and, during that time, she had two children and subsequently become divorced. When she came in, she explained that she had raised her two children mostly on her own, and both she and her children had very little contact with her ex-husband.

As is standard, we looked over the beneficiaries of her 401(k) (by far her largest account) and discovered that 100 percent of the proceeds (over $600,000) would have gone to her ex-husband had she passed away, and her children would have received nothing! She started to tear up, explaining she had a cancer scare a few years ago. Luckily, it had turned out okay, but, if she had passed away, it would have been devastating for the children to realize their mom's life savings would have gone to the estranged ex.

Trusts

Another piece of legacy planning to consider is the trust.

A trust is set up through an attorney and allows a third party, or trustee, to hold your assets and determine how they will pass to your beneficiaries. Many people are skeptical of trusts because they assume trusts are only appropriate for the fabulously wealthy.

However, a simple trust may only cost $1,000 to $2,500 in attorney's fees and can avoid both the expense and publicity of probate, provide a more immediate transfer of wealth, avoid some taxes, and provide you greater control over your legacy.[41]

For instance, if you want to set aside some funds for a grandchild's college education, you can make it a requirement he or she enrolls in classes before your trust will dispense any funds. Like a will, beneficiary lines will override your trust conditions, so you must still keep insurance policies and other assets up to date.

Like any financial or legal consideration, there are many options these days beyond the simple "yes or no" question of whether to have a trust. For one thing, you will need to consider if you want your trust to be revocable (you can change the terms while you are alive) or irrevocable (can't be changed; you are no longer the "owner" of the contents). A brief note here about irrevocable trusts: Although they have significant and greater tax benefits, they are still subject to a Medicaid look-back period. This means, if you transfer your assets into an irrevocable trust in an attempt to shelter them from a Medicaid spend-down, you will be ineligible for Medicaid coverage of long-term care for five years. Yet, an irrevocable trust can avoid both probate and estate taxes, and it can even protect assets from legal judgments against you.

Another thing to remember when it comes to trusts, in general, is, even if you have set up a trust, you must remember to fund it. In our years of work, we've had numerous clients come to us, assuming they have protected their assets with a trust. When we talk about taxes and other pieces of their legacy, it turns out they never retitled any assets or changed any paperwork on the assets they wanted in the trust. So,

---

[41] Regan Rondinelli-Haberek. LegalZoom. "What is the Average Cost to Prepare a Living Trust?" https://info.legalzoom.com/average-cost-prepare-living-trust-26932.html

please remember, a trust is just a bunch of fancy legal papers if you haven't followed through on retitling your assets.

Taxes

Although charitable contributions, trusts, and other tax-efficient strategies can reduce your tax bill, it's unlikely your estate will be passed on entirely tax-free. Yet, when it comes to building a legacy that can last for generations, taxes can be one of the heaviest drains on the impact of your hard work.

For 2017, the federal estate exemption was $5.49 million per individual and $10.98 million for a married couple, with estates facing up to a 40 percent tax rate after that. In 2020, those limits increased to $11.58 million for individuals and $23.16 million for married couples, with the 40 percent top level gift and estate tax remaining the same. Currently, the new estate limits are set to increase with inflation until January 1, 2026, when they will "sunset" back to the inflation-adjusted 2017 limits.[42, 43] And that's not taking into account the various state regulations and taxes regarding estate and inheritance transfers.

One "frequent flyer" of tax concerns: retirement accounts.

Your IRA or 401(k) can be a source of tax issues when you pass away. For one thing, taking funds from a sizeable account can trigger a large tax bill. However, if you leave the assets in the account, there are still required minimum distributions (RMDs), which will take effect even after you die. If you pass the account to your spouse, he or she can keep taking your RMDs as is, or your spouse can retitle the account in his or her

---

[42] Ashlea Ebeling. Forbes. December 21, 2018. "Final Tax Bill Includes Huge Estate Tax Win for the Rich: The $22.4 Million Exemption." https://www.forbes.com/sites/ashleaebeling/2017/12/21/final-tax-bill-includes-huge-estate-tax-win-for-the-rich-the-22-4-million-exemption/
[43] Ashlea Ebeling. Forbes. November 6, 2019. "IRS Announces Higher Estate and Gift Tax Limits For 2020." https://www.forbes.com/sites/ashleaebeling/2019/11/06/irs-announces-higher-estate-and-gift-tax-limits-for-2020/#18b9e5652efb

name and receive RMDs based on his or her life expectancy. Remember, if you don't take your RMDs, the IRS will take up to 50 percent of whatever your required distribution was, plus you will still have to pay income taxes whenever you withdraw that money. Thanks to rules enacted in 2020, anyone who inherits your IRA, with few exceptions (your spouse, a beneficiary less than ten years younger, or a disabled adult child, to name a few), will need to empty the account within ten years of your death.

Also—and this is a pretty big also—check with an attorney if you are considering putting your IRA or 401(k) in a trust. An improperly titled beneficiary form for the IRA could mean the difference of thousands of dollars in taxes. This is just one more reason to work with a financial professional, one who can strategically partner with an estate planning attorney to diligently check your decisions.

CHAPTER 9

Pensions

Pensions were once the foundation of a solid retirement income plan for many. These days, however, even as there are more investment vehicles, insurance options, and financial products available than ever before, pensions are an endangered species.

If you don't have a pension, read this paragraph, and then go ahead and skip to the next chapter (we'll save you some time here). Pensions are typically defined-benefit plans. Our employer pays in however much, and, if we work for that employer for a certain number of years (called the vestment period), we are entitled to a payout based on our salary and work history there. The benefit is the defined part—it's supposed to be income we can definitively count on in retirement. To supplement our pensions, or in the case of those without a pension, some of us are relying on what we believe are fundamentally unreliable or risk-laden assets, like stocks. As you near retirement, it may be in your best interest to consider how you might convert your more volatile assets into a guaranteed source of income.

From what our clients tell us, there is nothing more reassuring than knowing a check is coming in like clockwork every month. The peace of mind that comes from having a monthly check, whether from Social Security, a pension, an annuity, or any combination of those, is extremely comforting.

Since another check is coming in next month, most people don't feel bad about spending their income, knowing more will come in soon. For some who live off of market-based income only, we hear time and time again of the desire to pinch pennies in case of a downturn; this is why we don't recommend relying solely on the income generated from selling market-based instruments.

If you *do* have a pension, congratulations may be in order! This is the American *dream*! You know, a pension, an engraved watch, and riding out of cubicle life into a hazy sunset like a glorious retirement cowboy . . .

Whoa, there. Not so fast. Not to look a gift horse in the mouth, but perhaps we should at least check the shoes on this particular equine. Or, to overuse another metaphor, didn't your mother ever tell you not to put all your eggs in one basket? Diversifying the types of assets you own is a key part of planning your income in retirement. Pensions are no exception. The following are a few items on your checklist to keep in mind if you intend to be a proud pensioner down the road.

Check Funding

For one thing, there is a reason pensions have largely gone out of fashion. How well is your pension funded? Since the heyday of the pension, companies and governments have neglected to fund their pension obligations, creating a persistent problem with this otherwise reliable asset.

While open records laws make it pretty easy to know which government retirement systems have unfunded pension liabilities, private sector pensions haven't always had the same level of scrutiny. According to one report, the 200 biggest pension plans in the S&P 500 were underfunded by $240 billion in 2018.[44] Is your pension one of those?

---

44 Brandon Kochkodin. Bloomberg. April 11, 2019. "When a $240 Billion Corporate Pension Shortfall Is a Good Thing."

Every year, companies with private pension plans must file a Form 5500 with the federal government, so, if you work for a private company, checking up on your plan's health should be a matter of requesting the most recent Form 5500 from your plan administrator.[45]

Check the Fine Print

In addition to checking your pension's funding, be sure to read the fine print—just like any other financial contract, each company's pension has unique characteristics and options that could affect your retirement. For instance, your employer's plan may address inflation by tying income increases automatically to the national Consumer Price Index, by subjecting increases to a vote of a pension advisory board, or maybe by not even accounting for inflation at all. Similarly, some pensions have a provision to provide additional income in retirement if you become disabled. It's important, when you're building a financial strategy, to know what those various options are and how they might affect your income payout.

Spousal Options

If you are married, the fine print will need to extend beyond the page and into a discussion with your spouse. Typically, a pension has two options: *single* life and *joint* life. A single life pension will pay out for the life of the pension owner. It's a significantly larger monthly check, but the flipside is, should the pension owner die first, the remaining spouse will receive no further income from the pension. In contrast, a joint life

---

https://www.bloomberg.com/news/articles/2019-04-11/when-a-240-billion-corporate-pension-shortfall-is-a-good-thing

45 Pension Rights Center. "How Well-Funded is Your Pension Plan?" http://www.pensionrights.org/publications/fact-sheet/how-well-funded-your-pension-plan

pension is designed for the lifespan of both spouses. Although they will receive a smaller monthly check, that check won't stop coming until both spouses have died.

Here's another cautionary tale: Several years ago, a couple came in to see us about doing retirement planning. The husband, Jeff, was in his early seventies and his wife, Mary, was in her early sixties. Jeff retired eight years ago and had a pension. As we typically do, we looked into the pension option that was selected eight years ago. It was discovered that he selected the "single life only" pension option, meaning, when he passed away, the income stream would stop, and Mary would not receive a penny more. Obviously, he didn't intend to put his wife in a situation where she would have a shortfall of income if he passed away before her, but he didn't consult with a professional before making that decision. He only saw the highest monthly amount on the benefit selection form, and he chose that option, unaware of the implications. Needless to say, a decision as important to your future lifetime of income as this should be made with the full facts.

Check Your Trajectory

Another piece of the pension puzzle: Pensions aren't portable. Earlier, we mentioned there is a vesting period required in order to collect your pension. For baby boomers and their parents, this wasn't a problem—they didn't change jobs very frequently, and it wasn't unheard of for someone to work for a single employer for twenty years or more. Yet, the younger you are, the more likely you have worked several jobs in just the past decade.[46] This means, with each new generation, it gets less likely employees can last through the vestment period to even *qualify* for a pension, much less last long enough to have the company store up a significant value for

---

[46] Alison Doyle. The Balance. January 24, 2018. "How Often Do People Change Jobs?" https://www.thebalance.com/how-often-do-people-change-jobs-2060467

their retirement. So, particularly if you think you will consider a career—or just a company—change before retirement, be sure you're considering the fixed nature of your pension, plus any vesting period you'll have to face at a new company.

Check Your Options

If you have a pension, at some point you will be faced with the decision of how and when you'll begin taking payouts. *Before* the day you plan to ride off into the sunset, it is important to know the ins and outs of your pension.

What do we mean by "outs" of your pension? Well, as some companies and governments fall behind in their pension funding, one of the easiest ways to offload future obligations is for employers to ask employees to retire early and/or to take their pensions as a lump-sum/one-time payout instead of as guaranteed future income payments. Are you prepared for this possibility? Have you considered what you might do with that money (whether you're better off putting it in another product or sticking with the traditional pension), and have you discussed those things with a financial professional?

For many retirees with a pension plan, a lump-sum rollover might make more sense than the annuity options given by the pension plan. Some plans can produce more income from taking the pension's income options, but, for the majority of those we see, we can design a more appropriate and personalized strategy by using the lump-sum rollover provision.

First, the lump-sum is rolled over from the pension plan into an IRA, so it is a tax-free transaction. Taxes are only paid when funds are withdrawn from the IRA. Inside of the IRA, we can design a strategy to grow and distribute income as the client sees fit, instead of the take-it-or-leave-it options.

Save Elsewhere

Pensions were never meant to be the end-all-be-all of retirement, but with today's funding situation—or *under*funding situation—as a whole, they are no longer the firm foundation of financial preparations they were for older generations. So, no matter how well-funded your employer's pension plan is, you should be socking personal savings away in other places, whether in investments, insurance, or bank products.

Regardless of the particulars of your pension and its place in your financial strategies, these conversations should happen sooner rather than later. Our hope for you is that, the week before your retirement date, the most stressful decision you have is what kind of cake to serve at your retirement party.

CHAPTER 10

Finding a Financial Professional

For people nearing or in retirement, the professional with the greatest impact on your well-being, just short of your doctor, might very well be your financial advisor. The number one reason this is true is because mistakes can be costly. Moreover, as we get closer to retirement, the margin for error becomes smaller and smaller. Structuring a successful retirement hinges upon the coordination of important goals. Among these are having the right balance of risk in your retirement dollars, having enough income to provide a comfortable lifestyle, and achieving a reasonable rate of growth to keep pace with inflation.

Because your financial advisor can be so important to your enjoyment of retirement, it's wise to consider a few important key factors when selecting your advisor. Here are the three we believe are the most important to selecting an advisor so you can have confidence in your plan.

1. An advisor who does a written income plan. It's been said that those who write their goals down are most likely to achieve them. We believe this is true when it comes to preparing for retirement. We believe the number one key factor in determining retirement success is having a clearly written, solid game plan that addresses where your income will come from once retired—one balancing risk with return.

Everyone's situation is unique, so this plan shouldn't be "cookie-cutter." What separates the great planners from the rest is those who build a plan with your individual goals, objectives, and situation in mind.

Another two considerations when building a plan are how easy the plan is to follow and how many assumptions vs. guarantees are made. For example, if the plan is eighty pages long with two dozen different graphs and charts, and it seems like these don't make sense, what are the chances you will diligently follow this plan? More than likely, a highly complex plan will just look good in a binder for a day, and then it will be put on the shelf, never to be seen again until the next market downturn.

Next, if a plan assumes a consistently high rate of return without any market downturns or corrections, how likely is that plan to play out in the real world? For example, if a plan assumes a constant 6, 7, or even 8 percent return, there is a distinct possibility a market downturn somewhere in retirement will disrupt these assumptions. Risk and volatility can provide great buying opportunities during your working years, giving the ability to buy stocks or funds at a discount. But when you are retired and 1) more likely withdrawing money from your retirement accounts and 2) you won't have as much time to wait for the market to recover as you might have during your working years, then the market risk can present problems. For this reason, the plan should be built using a conservative rate of return or by building in as many guarantees as possible.

2. An advisor who is independent. You should be confident your advisor is on your team and has the ability and independence to implement solutions that fit your goals and needs. For this reason, we believe clients should strongly consider an independent advisor who can "shop around" the universe of strong financial companies to fit the client's individual goals. While a planner who works for only one financial institution might even understand your needs and goals, ultimately, they may only have a limited scope of solutions and could even have a financial incentive to recommend their firm's product, even when it might not be the best fit. We believe true independence means we work in the best interest of the client to develop a plan and then implement the solutions that best fit the individual client's needs—not the other way around.

3. An advisor who is relationship-driven. We believe it's of utmost importance to have a long-term relationship with an advisor. Life is fluid, and things will change and come up, both good and bad. If your relationship with an advisor is purely "transactional," such as just buying a product once and not staying in contact afterward, then this might not put you in the best position to be successful as things come up.

Important life events, such as parents passing away and leaving inheritances, children getting married and having grandchildren, downsizing or moving, health concerns, or just the financial markets changing, etc., will almost certainly come up in your lifetime. These important events make it crucial to have an advisor or team familiar with your personal situation who will give sound guidance based on those individual factors. When these updates and life events happen, it also makes sense to make changes in the context of an overall plan, rather than in a vacuum.

One thing is for sure: Life is very fluid and things will change. Everyone has their own individual and family dynamics they bring to the table. We believe you will be best served by advisors who truly put your long-term financial success and peace of mind first. But, a successful retirement is not dependent solely on finances. Family, health, travel, recreation, and other concerns ultimately come into the picture. A relationship with an advisor who will, both now and in the future, help you implement a plan that truly takes into consideration all of these things, and who will stay with you, is a blessing. In conclusion, a solid and well-thought-out plan with an advisor you trust is the recipe for ultimate peace of mind.

About the Authors

DAVID S. CORMAN
PRESIDENT OF GENERATIONS ADVISORY GROUP

David is focused on helping clients create workable solutions through seamless retirement income strategies and tireless dedication to a top-tier customer experience.

Since 1985, David has served over 5,000 families as a licensed insurance agent. In 2011, David founded Generations Advisory Group. His firm is dedicated to all aspects of retirement planning, including Social Security optimization, income planning, and investment planning. Generations also has an in-house affiliate law office. This model is truly a one-stop approach to help with the retirement planning needs of our clients.

In his free time, David enjoys cycling, sports, classic rock, and spending time with friends and family.

MATTHEW E. CORMAN
INVESTMENT ADVISER REPRESENTATIVE

Matthew is committed to working with clients towards their retirement goals by creating individualized retirement strategies. He is focused on helping with the creation, planning, and monitoring of client plans. Matthew has passed the Series 7 and 66 securities exams.

He joined his father at Generations Advisory Group in 2018 after a year of experience with another large firm. Matthew brought drive, determination, and focus with him to Generations Advisory Group. He is a graduate of Elon University. He is an avid Boston sports fan, and in his free time he enjoys traveling, eating Italian food, and golfing.

Made in United States
North Haven, CT
28 April 2022